Who Owns Intelligence?

AI Ownership, Accountability IP, and Copyright

From Data Rights and Control to Virtual Persons and Cognitary Guardianship

Dr Siamak Goudarzi

ISBN: 9798305326956

Dedication

For Bonnie, my daughter, whose eyes sparkle with curiosity and whose mind is a boundless source of wonder. May this book be a small contribution to the bright future you and your generation will shape, a future where AI serves humanity and enhances our lives.

Contents

About Author

Dr. Siamak Goudarzi is a distinguished lawyer, author, and thought leader at the forefront of the intersection between law, technology, and ethics. With over three decades of experience in the legal profession and an unwavering passion for exploring emerging technologies, Dr. Goudarzi has dedicated his career to addressing the profound questions posed by artificial intelligence (AI) and its transformative impact on society.

Dr. Goudarzi is the author of several critically acclaimed books that push the boundaries of thought and inquiry:

- *AI for Legal Professionals: A Fast and Intelligent Partner in Precision and Performance*, where he explores how AI is revolutionizing the legal field, empowering professionals with tools to enhance efficiency, precision, and client service.
- *The Emergence of Virtual Persons: A Legal and Ethical Framework for AI and Robot Rights*, a groundbreaking work that investigates the legal and ethical challenges posed by increasingly autonomous AI systems, introducing concepts that have sparked global conversations about AI personhood and the future of accountability.
- *Awakening Intelligence: Criteria for Sentient AI*, which delves into the biological, philosophical, and ethical dimensions of AI sentience. By proposing a thoughtful framework, Dr. Goudarzi examines what it means for machines to achieve consciousness and how society should navigate this monumental transformation.
- *Beyond Algorithms: Exploring the Intersection of Artificial Intelligence and Spirituality*, a thought-provoking work that examines how age-old spiritual questions of meaning, transcendence, and interconnectedness intersect with AI, offering a unique perspective on humanity's evolving relationship with intelligent technology.

In this work, *Who Owns Intelligence?: AI Ownership, Accountability IP, and Copyright* Dr. Goudarzi tackles one of the most pressing challenges in AI today: the ownership of AI-generated works and the boundaries of control over intelligent systems. Building on his earlier introduction of *Virtual Persons*, he debuts the innovative concept of *Cognitary Guardianship* (CG), a framework that redefines AI and robot "ownership" by positioning humans as guardians rather than outright owners. In this deeply expanded edition, Dr. Goudarzi addresses the complexities of AI outputs—such as inventions and creative works—that challenge traditional intellectual property norms. By weaving in global regulatory experiments and diverse cultural perspectives, he highlights the urgent need for forward-thinking policies that balance technological innovation with human oversight and accountability.

Dr. Goudarzi's unique blend of legal expertise, philosophical inquiry, and technological insight drives his work to the leading edge of AI discourse. Whether examining AI's practical roles in professional sectors, probing the conceptual underpinnings of personhood, or exploring the spiritual dimensions of intelligent technology, he consistently pushes beyond conventional boundaries. His writings encourage scholars, practitioners, and the public to grapple with the ethical, legal, and societal transformations brought about by AI—ultimately shaping the conversations that will define how humanity and intelligent machines coexist in the decades to come.

Preface

The concept of ownership has long been a cornerstone of legal, ethical, and economic systems. From the dawn of civilization, humanity has sought to categorize and control the world around it—assigning ownership to objects, land, inventions, and even intangible ideas. Yet, as technology accelerates at an unprecedented pace, the notion of ownership is being profoundly disrupted. Nowhere is this disruption more evident than in the realm of artificial intelligence (AI), where tools are no longer merely extensions of human effort but are beginning to operate with a degree of autonomy and agency.

For many years, I have found myself grappling with this reality at the intersection of law, technology, and ethics. My previous works, *AI for Legal Professionals* and *The Emergence of Virtual Persons*, examined the transformative power of AI within legal frameworks and the ethical dilemmas posed by increasingly autonomous systems. *AI for Legal Professionals* underscored AI's capacity to boost precision and productivity, while exposing its limitations as a straightforward tool. *The Emergence of Virtual Persons* ventured further, probing how highly adaptive AI systems—those capable of learning, self-modifying, and making decisions—might challenge traditional definitions of legal personhood. From these explorations sprang a deeper question: Can entities that learn, adapt, and operate autonomously truly be owned? When intelligence begins to exhibit qualities akin to human agency, the notion of "ownership" grows strained—forcing us to reconsider longstanding assumptions about control, liability, and moral accountability.

It was this realization that led me to write *Who Owns Intelligence?: A Legal and Ethical Guide to Rethinking AI Ownership*. In earlier debates, Joanna Bryson (2010) famously proposed that "robots should be slaves," contending that AI systems must remain firmly under human dominion to maintain clear lines of responsibility. Other scholars, including Ryan Abbott and Jacob Turner, have shown how AI-generated content, from patents to creative works, is already testing the boundaries of current legal frameworks. While Bryson cautioned against diluting human accountability by granting AI any form of personhood, my own inquiries into the notion of "Virtual Persons" (Goudarzi, 2024) suggested a different dilemma: Are there AI systems so adaptive and autonomous that treating them as mere property no longer makes sense?

In this book, I introduce a groundbreaking idea: Cognitary Guardianship (CG). Coined and elaborated here for the first time, CG poses a radically different approach from either strict property-based models or full-fledged AI personhood. It positions humans as guardians—responsible stewards with ethical and legal obligations to oversee AI that may learn and act with considerable independence. Cognitary Guardianship aims to protect the core principle of human responsibility while acknowledging that advanced AI can, under certain conditions, transcend the constraints of being a "mere tool." Yet this proposal raises an array of questions—legal, moral, and practical—that demand careful scrutiny.

Over the course of fifteen chapters, this book examines how AI's growing autonomy unsettles the bedrock of ownership. Early discussions consider the tension between existing intellectual property laws and autonomous AI outputs, while later chapters explore experimental regulatory regimes worldwide, as well as alternative frameworks like stewardship, custodial agency, and co-agency. Expanding upon earlier drafts, new chapters (11 through 15) delve into the intricate ownership vacuum for AI-generated works, the evolving challenges in patent, trademark, and copyright law, and the global efforts—ranging from Europe to Asia—to reconcile AI's promise with public accountability. Throughout these chapters, the idea of Cognitary Guardianship gains definition as a practical, if provocative, means of bridging the gulf between AI's potential and the ethical imperatives of human oversight.

This book is not merely theoretical; it grapples with the real-world implications of AI's evolution. From generative models that produce original art to autonomous vehicles making instantaneous life-and-death decisions, AI is altering industries, careers, and individual lives. The following questions emerge as both urgent and inescapable: Who owns the outputs of an autonomous AI? What happens when AI systems behave unpredictably or beyond direct human control? What responsibilities do we, as creators, users, or guardians, hold for these technologies? And how can we ensure that as AI grows in power, it remains anchored in a framework that respects human values and ethical norms?

This book is an invitation to reflect on these dilemmas, whether you approach them from the perspective of an AI developer, a legal scholar, a policymaker, or a curious reader pondering the future of intelligence. We stand at the brink of a transformation where boundaries of ownership, personhood, and agency are being reconfigured in ways that may alter our collective trajectory for generations. By proposing Cognitary Guardianship, I hope to offer not a final answer but a viable starting point for debate and action—a framework that strives to balance innovation and accountability, progress and ethics.

The chapters that follow are intended to spark dialogue and guide us toward a more thoughtful engagement with AI's rapidly unfolding capabilities. As we shape the future of intelligent machines, we must do so with care, recognizing that our responses to these challenges will help define not only the status of AI, but our own humanity in relation to the technology we create. Let us proceed wisely, acknowledging both the promise and the peril of an era in which AI systems are no longer mere reflections of human effort, but evolving partners—and, in some cases, wards—necessitating robust ethical and legal stewardship.

Introduction

Artificial Intelligence has transitioned from a speculative idea to a transformative force shaping our world, influencing everything from medical diagnostics and creative arts to autonomous vehicles and humanoid robotics. With AI systems now capable of learning, adapting, and functioning autonomously, the question of who owns intelligence—and whether intelligence can or should even be "owned"—has become one of the most pressing legal, ethical, and societal challenges of our time. As this book demonstrates, the evolution of AI demands that we revisit deeply held assumptions about property, liability, and responsibility, and consider innovative frameworks for governing entities that may not neatly fit into categories of "persons" or "things."

Traditionally, legal frameworks have been built around clear distinctions: tools are owned, people are not. Intellectual property laws protect outputs such as inventions, artistic creations, and writings, while liability models hold human agents accountable for the actions of tools, machines, and systems under their control. But what happens when the "tool" exhibits autonomy, unpredictability, and the ability to make decisions independent of human oversight? Is the concept of ownership, as it has long been understood, still relevant in a world where AI systems can operate and even innovate with limited human input?

Joanna Bryson (2010) famously argued that "robots should be slaves," contending that AI systems must remain tools under strict human control to avoid dehumanizing people or diluting accountability. Bryson warns that any form of "personhood" for AI risks shifting moral and legal responsibilities away from humans, where she believes they firmly belong. By contrast, emerging scholarship—exemplified by Dr. Siamak Goudarzi's *The Emergence of Virtual Persons* (2024)—challenges this tool-based paradigm, suggesting that due to their autonomy and learning capabilities, some AI systems may warrant recognition as "Virtual Persons." These systems, Goudarzi argues, inhabit a grey zone between property and legal personhood and demand new approaches to governance.

In response to these complexities, this book introduces a novel concept called **Cognitary Guardianship**. Coined and elaborated here for the first time, Cognitary Guardianship (CG) reimagines AI's legal and ethical standing. Rather than classifying AI as mere property or advocating for its full-fledged personhood, CG treats AI as a ward requiring ethical oversight and deliberate governance. By situating humans as "guardians" instead of absolute owners, Cognitary Guardianship preserves accountability and human responsibility even as AI evolves toward greater autonomy, thereby offering a balanced solution to the conundrum of AI ownership.

Such tension between strict tool-based frameworks and more radical proposals like AI personhood underscores a profound dilemma: if AI reaches a stage where it exhibits near-human levels of autonomy and agency, can it be reduced to a piece of property with a simple "owned–not owned" status? Or do we need alternative paradigms—like Cognitary Guardianship, co-agency, stewardship, or custodial agency—that move beyond ownership while preserving the lines of human responsibility?

These questions also intersect with the broader global conversation around AI rights and legal personhood. The European Parliament's 2017 discussion on "electronic personhood" brought international attention to whether granting AI some legal status might ensure transparency and accountability, even as critics cautioned against blurring the boundaries between human and non-human entities. Nations like Japan and South Korea have meanwhile launched experiments in AI policy, underscoring the diversity of regulatory perspectives worldwide. Some jurisdictions, as this book later explores, have even contemplated limited IP rights for AI-generated works—opening further debate on whether AI can or should "own" anything at all (Matulionyte & Lee, 2021).

Building on multiple disciplines—law, philosophy, ethics, economics, and technology—this book aims to tackle the pivotal questions of our time:

- Who owns the outputs of AI systems—such as inventions, artistic works, and algorithmic decisions?
- If an AI acts independently, who (or what) should bear the consequences of its actions and decisions?
- Should advanced AI be considered property, partners, or even legal entities, particularly if they develop features akin to autonomy?
- Can Cognitary Guardianship provide a balanced, sustainable framework for AI governance?

In addressing these questions, the text now spans fifteen chapters (plus a concluding overview), reflecting a more comprehensive treatment of emerging issues around AI-generated content, regulatory experimentation, and global governance concerns:

1. **Chapter 1** introduces the fundamental question of AI ownership, setting the stage for the complex debates to follow.
2. **Chapter 2** examines the foundations and limitations of existing intellectual property laws in addressing AI-driven innovation.
3. **Chapter 3** explores control, liability, and the inadequacy of traditional "tool-based" paradigms in managing increasingly autonomous AI systems.
4. **Chapter 4** delves into evolving ideas of personhood, including policy experiments on AI autonomy.
5. **Chapter 5** challenges binary thinking by presenting a nuanced spectrum of autonomy and agency in AI.
6. **Chapter 6** formally introduces Cognitary Guardianship (CG) as a novel conceptual framework proposed by the author, highlighting its distinctions from both tool-based and personhood approaches.
7. **Chapter 7** broadens the conversation by analyzing alternative ownership frameworks such as stewardship, custodial agency, and co-agency models.
8. **Chapter 8** provides a global perspective on AI regulation, examining international approaches and experimental policies that reflect divergent legal philosophies.
9. **Chapter 9** reimagines ownership paradigms in the context of virtual persons, suggesting ways in which AI autonomy compels us to rethink conventional notions of property.
10. **Chapter 10** concludes the initial series of debates by offering actionable policy recommendations and proposing forward-looking pathways in AI governance.
11. **Chapter 11** shifts the spotlight to the "ownership vacuum" that arises when AI-generated works lack a clear human creator, creating novel legal and ethical ambiguities.
12. **Chapter 12** explores the broader intellectual property challenges posed by AI, from patent inventorship to trademark disputes, situating these issues within the global push to reform IP law.
13. **Chapter 13** focuses on copyright ownership in generative AI, discussing who, if anyone, can claim rights over machine-generated art, music, text, or designs that involve minimal human oversight.

14. **Chapter 14** examines additional ownership models—co-agency, custodial agency, stewardship, and cognitary guardianship—while detailing how each might address the complexities of AI-driven innovation.
15. **Chapter 15** investigates regulatory approaches and policy pathways, synthesizing national and international initiatives to harmonize AI governance, address ethical considerations, and ensure that AI's integration remains transparent and accountable.

A final Conclusion ties these discussions together, emphasizing the urgent need for rethinking both ownership and accountability as AI becomes more enmeshed in daily life, public systems, and market forces.

While the book concludes with a comprehensive Glossary of Key Terms and References, the overarching narrative points to a world in which AI's capacity to learn and act autonomously challenges the very foundations of conventional legal theories. By the time readers reach the final pages, they will have encountered contrasting models—ranging from strict tool-based views to emergent personhood debates, from straightforward ownership claims to hybrid guardianship paradigms—and seen how each offers a partial but potentially incomplete picture of AI's unfolding role in society.

As AI continues to evolve, our willingness to question the premise of "ownership" may be crucial to ensuring that these systems are developed and deployed in ways that respect human values and social well-being. Whether one embraces Cognitary Guardianship, explores co-agency, or aligns with Bryson's (2010) insistence on maintaining AI as tool-like "slaves," the debates in this book signal that the stakes are nothing less than the ethical scaffolding of our future. Each chapter invites scholars, policymakers, technologists, and the broader public to engage in a conversation that transcends any single discipline, recognizing that how we classify and regulate AI will profoundly shape the coming decades, not just for technology, but for humanity itself.

Chapter 1: AI and the Question of Ownership

Initially, AI systems were designed for narrow, specific tasks—commonly referred to as Artificial Narrow Intelligence (ANI). These systems excelled in tightly controlled domains, such as language translation, image recognition, and playing strategy games like chess or Go. However, their abilities were confined to predefined tasks, lacking the adaptability and reasoning capacity required to address broader, more complex challenges (Soroosh, 2023).

The evolution of AI has been marked by periods of rapid progress interspersed with periods of disillusionment and stagnation, often referred to as 'AI winters.' These periods of setback have often been followed by breakthroughs in areas like machine learning, deep learning, and neural networks, driving renewed interest and investment in AI research.

In recent years, however, the development of autonomous systems capable of learning, decision-making, and adaptation has marked a profound shift toward what some describe as Artificial General Intelligence (AGI). Unlike ANI, AGI holds the potential to perform tasks across domains, mimicking the cognitive abilities of humans. This emerging shift introduces entirely new paradigms of AI autonomy and agency, where systems no longer merely "assist" humans but operate independently with the capacity to evolve their knowledge and behavior (IABAC, 2023).

More recent advancements, including agentic AI, illustrate this evolution further. Agentic AI systems demonstrate the ability to complete multi-step tasks, make decisions without ongoing human input, and collaborate with other systems to achieve complex goals. For example, autonomous vehicles navigate unpredictable environments, while language models generate creative works and simulate decision-making processes traditionally confined to humans (Analytics Insight, 2023). This accelerating development raises a critical question that lies at the heart of this book: Who owns intelligence when it operates with a degree of independence and agency?

True AI agency, however, remains a subject of ongoing debate. While some AI systems can exhibit autonomous behavior and make seemingly independent decisions, true agency would require consciousness, self-awareness, and the ability to set and pursue its own goals, which remains largely within the realm of philosophical speculation.

Rethinking Ownership: Virtual Persons and Beyond

At the core of this discussion is the concept of ownership itself. Traditional legal systems have always drawn a clear line between tools and persons. Tools, whether machines, vehicles, or software, are treated as property—owned, controlled, and used by human agents. Persons, on the other hand, are legal entities with certain rights and responsibilities, including the ability to own property.

However, as AI systems evolve, they increasingly challenge this dichotomy. Scholars like Goudarzi (2024), in The Emergence of Virtual Persons, argue for the recognition of Virtual Persons—a novel category of legal entities that exist in the space between tools and traditional legal persons. Virtual Persons are autonomous AI systems with the capacity to operate independently, make decisions, and produce outcomes that cannot be attributed directly to human intervention. While these systems do not possess consciousness or sentience, their unique blend of autonomy and functionality challenges the current legal paradigms of ownership and accountability (Goudarzi, 2024).

This challenge raises key tensions:

- Ownership of AI Outputs vs. AI Systems: Who owns the outcomes—art, inventions, or decisions—produced by an AI system? Can ownership be extended to the AI entity itself, as one would with software, or does its autonomy make this problematic?
- Accountability and Agency: If an AI system operates independently and unpredictably, to whom do we attribute liability or moral responsibility? Does the human owner bear accountability, or must we redefine what it means to "control" such systems?
- Legal and Ethical Limits: As AI approaches human-like functionality, does treating it purely as property diminish our ethical responsibilities?

The increasing autonomy of AI systems raises concerns about potential biases and discrimination. If AI systems are trained on biased data or designed with inherent biases, they can perpetuate and even amplify existing societal inequalities. Ensuring fairness, transparency, and accountability in AI development and deployment is crucial to mitigate these risks.

Key Terms in the AI Ownership Debate

To navigate this evolving landscape, it is essential to clarify the key terms that form the foundation of this book's discussion on AI ownership, responsibility, and regulation. While many of these terms have appeared in academic or industry dialogues, their precise meanings often vary across disciplines and jurisdictions. The following definitions provide a shared framework for understanding the complexities addressed in subsequent chapters.

Virtual Persons (Goudarzi, 2024)
Autonomous AI entities with independent decision-making capabilities, as first conceptualized by Dr. Siamak Goudarzi in *The Emergence of Virtual Persons* (2024). Although these systems do not possess full sentience, their ability to learn, adapt, and exert influence on human environments necessitates a rethinking of their legal and ethical status beyond that of a simple tool.

AI-Generated Works (HCR Law, 2023)
Creations—such as inventions, music, art, or decisions—produced by AI systems. Legal systems globally remain divided on who, if anyone, "owns" such outputs. Some jurisdictions suggest that rights belong to AI's creators or users, while others question whether AI outputs fit within the traditional framework of human-authored works.

Data Rights (The Barrister Group, 2023)
The legal and ethical considerations around data collection, ownership, usage, and privacy, particularly when training AI models on large datasets. Issues of consent, fair compensation, and protection become more complex as AI expands into domains that involve personal, proprietary, or culturally sensitive data.

Intellectual Property (IP) (Ashurst, 2022)
A traditional legal framework for protecting inventions and creative works, encompassing patents, copyrights, and trademarks. Current IP laws focus

primarily on human creators, leaving unresolved questions about AI-generated outputs and how they fit into notions of originality, inventorship, and authorship.

Cognitary Guardianship (Proposed in This Book)
A concept introduced here as an alternative to conventional ownership. Cognitary Guardianship treats AI systems neither as mere property nor as fully autonomous "persons," but rather as wards for which humans serve as stewards or guardians. This model seeks to preserve accountability and ethical oversight by assigning legal responsibility to humans, while acknowledging AI's growing capacity for independent action.

AI Personhood
The broader debate on granting AI systems limited legal rights and obligations, akin to those assigned to corporations or other non-human entities. Supporters argue that AI personhood might streamline liability and accountability for complex AI behaviors; critics worry that it could dilute human moral responsibilities or create legal loopholes (Matulionyte & Lee, 2021).

Algorithmic Bias
Systematic errors in AI systems that produce unfair or discriminatory outcomes. Bias may arise from skewed training data or from unintentional design choices, disproportionately impacting certain groups and undermining trust in AI decision-making (Springer, 2020).

Transparency
The ability to understand how an AI system arrives at its decisions, as well as the data it uses. Calls for transparency reflect the need to ensure that AI-driven processes can be audited, verified, and held accountable by regulators and the public (World Economic Forum, 2024).

Explainability
Closely related to transparency, explainability focuses on providing understandable justifications for AI outputs. For instance, an explainable AI system might reveal the factors or weightings used to generate a medical diagnosis or a credit assessment, thus facilitating oversight and recourse in cases of error or bias.

Accountability
The responsibility to prevent or address harm arising from AI systems. This term underscores the importance of identifying and enforcing obligations—whether on developers, deployers, or "guardians"—to manage, correct, or compensate for wrongful AI actions (NatLawReview, 2024).

Ethical AI
AI designed, developed, and implemented with considerations of fairness, safety, and societal well-being at the forefront. Ethical AI initiatives aim to prevent algorithmic bias, protect privacy, and maintain human oversight over autonomous decision-making processes (Deloitte, 2024).

Stewardship
The responsible management and care of AI systems, emphasizing ethical and sustainable oversight rather than mere possession. Stewards ensure that AI technologies serve the common good, comply with legal norms, and respect human values.

Custodial Agency
A governance model whereby a human or organization acts as a custodian for AI systems, bearing fiduciary responsibility for their decisions and impacts. Similar to Cognitary Guardianship, but more focused on centralized control and often tied to specific licenses or legal mandates.

Co-Agency
A collaborative framework in which humans and AI systems jointly participate in decision-making. Instead of assigning sole ownership or accountability to either party, co-agency recognizes that both humans and intelligent machines contribute expertise and perspectives, raising novel questions about how to share benefits, risks, and responsibilities.

Superintelligence
A speculative level of AI surpassing human intelligence across all domains, including creativity, problem-solving, and broad reasoning. Though not yet realized, the prospect of superintelligent AI raises existential questions about humanity's ability to maintain oversight and moral responsibility (Futurium, 2023).

Singularity
The hypothetical point at which technological growth becomes uncontrollable and irreversible, often linked to the advent of superintelligent AI. Debates over the Singularity revolve around whether human institutions can remain relevant once machines learn and evolve on exponential timescales (OUP, 2024).

By defining these terms, we establish a baseline for understanding the multifaceted debates in subsequent chapters. The question of AI ownership intersects with ethical considerations, global policy challenges, evolving legal frameworks, and ongoing philosophical discussions over what it means to create—and to be responsible for—an increasingly autonomous form of intelligence.

The ownership of AI systems and their outputs will have profound social and economic consequences. The concentration of AI ownership in the hands of a few powerful entities could exacerbate existing inequalities, while widespread access to AI tools could empower individuals and communities. Careful consideration of these societal impacts is essential to ensure that the benefits of AI are distributed equitably.

To address the complex ethical challenges posed by AI, the establishment of independent AI Ethics Boards could play a crucial role. These boards, comprised of experts from diverse fields such as law, ethics, philosophy, and technology, could provide guidance and oversight on the development and deployment of AI systems, ensuring that ethical considerations are prioritized at every stage.

Why This Question Matters

The ownership of AI systems and their outputs has far-reaching implications for society. As technologies evolve, traditional frameworks are proving inadequate to address the complex ethical, economic, and legal challenges that arise. For example, the UK's Copyright, Designs, and Patents Act (CDPA, 1988) attributes authorship of computer-generated works to the individual or entity that made the necessary arrangements for the creation of the work. However, this provision is increasingly strained as AI systems demonstrate creativity and adaptability without human direction (A&O Shearman, 2023).

Moreover, the economic and societal stakes are immense. The integration of AI into industries such as healthcare, finance, and transportation has already begun to shift power dynamics and redefine human labor. Questions about ownership and control are not merely academic—they influence how wealth, accountability, and innovation are distributed globally.

A Multidisciplinary Approach to AI Ownership

Addressing the complexities of AI ownership requires more than a single lens or expertise; it demands a convergence of insights from multiple fields to capture the full breadth of legal, ethical, economic, philosophical, and technological challenges. By weaving together perspectives from law, philosophy, ethics, economics, and technology, this book charts a path that acknowledges not only the theoretical dimensions of ownership but also the very real-world implications that AI introduces. Each discipline contributes unique methodologies, questions, and principles, yielding a holistic framework for navigating the uncertainties of AI in our rapidly evolving world.

Law
Legal scholarship and practice provide the foundational structures for discussing property rights, intellectual property (IP) protections, and liability principles (Ashurst, 2022). Historically, these frameworks have assumed that creations—be they inventions or artistic works—stem from identifiable human authors or inventors, and that tools remain firmly under human control. Yet AI challenges these assumptions by generating outputs with minimal or no human intervention, and by operating in ways that defy straightforward command-and-control paradigms (HCR Law, 2023). Legal debates also touch on enforcement mechanisms across jurisdictions, highlighting tensions between national approaches (NatLawReview, 2024) and underscoring the need for international cooperation to mitigate legal uncertainties (World Economic Forum, 2024).

Philosophy
Philosophical inquiry underlies core questions about autonomy, agency, and personhood—concepts that become especially urgent when AI displays emergent behavior or creativity (Springer, 2020). Philosophy challenges us to consider whether AI, as a non-human entity, could ever

possess moral or legal standing. Should we attribute "intent" or "authorship" to a system whose operations, though powerful, remain fundamentally algorithmic? Grappling with these considerations reframes debates about AI ownership into more profound reflections on consciousness, meaning, and the human experience (OUP, 2024).

Ethics
Ethical theory connects the abstract inquiries of philosophy with actionable guidelines for responsible AI development and deployment (Deloitte, 2024). Discussions center on accountability and fairness, urging designers and policymakers to embed transparency, explainability, and safety into AI systems from the earliest stages (IEEE, 2024). Ethics also interrogates the societal impact of AI ownership. For instance, if large corporations dominate AI patents or data, how does that affect global equity, workforce well-being, and the protection of vulnerable groups? By placing human values at the core, ethics compels us to reevaluate not only what we own but how we wield that ownership in the broader social context.

Economics
Economic analysis explains how AI ownership will influence incentives, value creation, and the distribution of wealth and power. AI systems can revolutionize productivity, especially when companies leverage proprietary algorithms or data to gain competitive advantages (OECD, 2020). At the same time, concerns arise about labor displacement, monopolization, and rising inequality if ownership of AI-generated outputs remains concentrated among a few actors. Economists highlight the importance of balanced markets and robust regulatory frameworks to ensure that AI-driven innovations benefit society at large, rather than amplifying existing disparities (The Barrister Group, 2023).

Technology
Technical understanding provides the grounding for all other dimensions of AI ownership. AI's capabilities—such as the ability to learn from vast datasets, adapt strategies in real time, and generate creative outputs—stem from developments in machine learning, neural networks, and algorithm design (Weber et al., 2020). Appreciating the technical underpinnings clarifies why traditional IP notions may falter, as well as why concepts like fiduciary duty or guardianship must adapt to keep pace with increasingly autonomous, data-intensive AI applications. Technology also offers

potential solutions, including algorithmic auditing, data provenance tracking, and transparent system architectures that facilitate accountability and cross-border cooperation (IEEE Spectrum, 2024).

By integrating these perspectives, a multidisciplinary approach illuminates not merely how AI ownership challenges existing norms, but also why those challenges demand urgent policy attention. Legal frameworks ensure enforcement, yet they must contend with philosophical notions of agency; ethical considerations guide design choices, but economics shapes the incentives that drive AI innovation; and without technical expertise, proposals for AI governance may remain disconnected from the practical realities of how AI systems operate. Only through this synergistic lens can society develop robust, future-proof solutions for managing ownership in an era when AI is set to transform not just our economies, but also the very fabric of human creativity, autonomy, and co-existence.

By bridging these diverse fields, this book aims to provide a comprehensive analysis of AI ownership, challenging existing frameworks and introducing innovative models such as Cognitary Guardianship. The chapters that follow will explore the legal, ethical, and philosophical questions that arise as AI systems continue to evolve. We begin by examining how traditional intellectual property laws and liability models fall short in the face of AI's growing autonomy, and why new frameworks are urgently needed to govern this unprecedented technological transformation.

Chapter 2: Intellectual Property Foundations and Limitations

In the wake of rapid advancements in machine learning and autonomous systems, legal, ethical, and technological debates increasingly focus on the ownership and authorship of AI-generated content. Historically, Intellectual Property (IP) frameworks were designed to protect human creativity and innovation by granting exclusive rights to individuals or organizations responsible for producing original works. Yet these frameworks—codified in laws governing copyrights, patents, and trademarks—are being challenged by AI systems that can autonomously craft text, music, art, and even patents, often with minimal or no direct human input.

Central to this discussion are the writings of scholars like Ryan Abbott and Mark A. Lemley, who have examined how AI-driven invention unsettles key assumptions underlying IP law. Abbott (2016), for instance, argues that patent law—which traditionally rewards human ingenuity—fails to accommodate machine inventors, leaving courts and policymakers unsure of how (or whether) to assign inventorship to non-human entities. Lemley (2020) similarly explores the notion of AI-generated content and the difficulties in attributing authorship, highlighting that IP regimes founded on human creativity provide an imperfect fit when the "creator" is a learning algorithm rather than an individual with a discernible moral and economic interest.

Even where humans are nominally "in the loop," many modern AI systems learn and iterate on data in ways that escape simple claims of direct human authorship. Creative outputs thus challenge established notions of originality, since the AI's data-driven processes may remix or replicate existing works, raising complex questions about infringement, fair use, and the true "inventor" or "author." As these challenges mount, courts and legal bodies worldwide are grappling with whether an AI's outputs can or should be accorded the same protections as human-generated works, and if so, who reaps the rewards or bears the liabilities.

Against this backdrop, it is becoming clear that while current IP frameworks offer robust protection for human-generated material, they are not fully equipped to address the complexities inherent in autonomous AI systems. Whether it is the copyright landscape—where originality and the "human author" concept hold sway—or patent law—where inventorship is predicated on demonstrable human ingenuity—questions remain unanswered. These gaps underscore the growing consensus that novel approaches may be necessary, including models like Cognitary Guardianship, which propose assigning ethical and legal stewardship for AI to humans without conflating AI systems themselves with human creators.

Historically, IP laws have presumed a human creator at the heart of any protected work. Whether an artist painting a masterpiece or an inventor designing a groundbreaking product, the law has always associated ownership with a human originator. AI challenges this assumption. Autonomous systems today can generate novels, compose symphonies, design architectural blueprints, and even invent solutions to technical problems—all without direct human input.

For example, generative AI systems like OpenAI's GPT models and DeepMind's AlphaFold demonstrate capabilities that rival, and in some cases surpass, human expertise in producing original and complex outputs (Lemley, 2023). These developments expose critical gaps in existing IP laws, raising questions such as:

- Who owns an AI-generated work when no human can claim authorship?
- Should ownership default to the AI developer, the end-user, or no one at all?
- Can an AI entity itself be granted rights over its outputs, and if so, what would that mean for traditional notions of IP?

Overview of Intellectual Property Laws and Their Applicability to AI Outputs

Intellectual Property (IP) law serves as a foundational mechanism for encouraging innovation, protecting creative investments, and fostering fair competition. Traditionally, IP frameworks focus on **human** inventors, authors, and brand owners, granting them exclusive rights in exchange for making their discoveries or creations publicly known. As AI systems develop the capacity to generate everything from music and art to novel inventions, however, these established regimes face new dilemmas: Where does ownership reside if the "creative mind" behind a work is non-human?

The primary categories of IP—**copyrights**, **patents**, and **trademarks**—offer unique avenues of protection, each with its own complexities when applied to AI-generated content:

1. **Copyrights**
   Copyright laws protect original literary, artistic, and creative works, granting authors exclusive rights to reproduce, distribute, and display these works. In most jurisdictions, copyright attaches automatically upon the work's creation, without the need for formal registration (U.S. Copyright Office, 2023). However, the traditional assumption that a "human author" stands behind each creation becomes tenuous when an AI autonomously produces text, music, or images.
   - **Human Authorship vs. Autonomous Creation**: Courts and administrative bodies, including the U.S. Copyright Office, have repeatedly ruled that purely machine-generated works without human input do not qualify for copyright (U.S. Copyright Office, 2023). This leaves unanswered questions about the threshold of human involvement needed to claim rights, especially in scenarios where AI refines, edits, or synthesizes data originally provided by humans.
   - **Fair Use and Data Concerns**: AI systems often rely on massive datasets that may include copyrighted material. While some developers claim fair use for training data, others argue that large-scale data scraping constitutes infringement, fueling debates over whether machine outputs derived from these datasets are "transformative" or simply repurposing existing works (Matulionyte & Lee, 2021).

2. **Patents**
   Patents grant inventors the exclusive right to make, use, or sell their inventions for a specified period, typically 20 years from the filing date. Historically, patent law is predicated on human ingenuity, rewarding individuals or entities that demonstrate novelty, non-obviousness, and utility.
   - **Human Inventorship vs. AI Innovators**: Recent high-profile cases (e.g., *Thaler v. Comptroller-General of Patents, Designs and Trade Marks*) have tested the boundaries of patent law by naming AI systems as inventors (Matulionyte

& Lee, 2021). Most courts have rejected these applications, insisting on the necessity of human inventorship. This stance leaves open the question of who (if anyone) owns an invention conceptualized primarily by an AI system operating beyond direct human commands.

- o **Disclosure and Enablement**: Patent law mandates a detailed disclosure sufficient for skilled individuals to replicate the invention. When AI's "inventive step" emerges from opaque deep-learning processes, fulfilling disclosure requirements can be challenging—leading policymakers to debate whether specialized rules are needed for AI-driven inventions (Abbott, 2016).

3. **Trademarks**

   Trademarks protect words, symbols, and designs used to distinguish goods or services in the marketplace. They ensure that consumers can identify and trust specific brands, shielding brand owners from unauthorized use that might create confusion.

   - o **AI-Generated Branding and Consumer Confusion**: An AI might generate logos, slogans, or brand designs autonomously. If these outputs resemble existing trademarks, questions arise regarding infringement and liability. Who bears responsibility if an AI inadvertently produces branding that conflicts with established marks?
   - o **Evolving Standards of Originality**: Trademarks hinge more on distinctiveness and consumer recognition than on originality per se (Ashurst, 2022). Nonetheless, if AI outputs are so closely inspired by existing marks as to create confusion, the trademark holder might pursue claims of infringement—leaving courts to assess the AI's role versus the role of the human who deployed it.

Challenges Posed by AI to IP Frameworks

1. **Authorship and Ownership**

   AI challenges the assumption that a single, identifiable human creator or inventor stands behind each work. In many AI-driven projects, multiple stakeholders—developers, data contributors, users offering prompts—can lay partial claim to the final output, complicating rights and responsibilities.

2. **Liability and Enforcement**
   Traditional IP enforcement mechanisms rely on identifying a human or corporate entity that infringed or misused protected material. If an AI system autonomously generates infringing content, it remains unclear whether the AI's developer, the user, or both should be held liable (NatLawReview, 2024).
3. **Data Privacy and Ethical Use**
   As AI systems digest vast amounts of personal or proprietary data to generate outputs, questions about licensing, consent, and ethical data mining come to the fore. Privacy advocates argue that existing data protections were not designed for large-scale AI training, necessitating updates to laws like the EU's GDPR or new guidance on data usage (World Economic Forum, 2024).
4. **Global Fragmentation**
   IP laws vary substantially across jurisdictions. Some nations emphasize strict requirements for human authorship, while others explore more flexible definitions of authorship or inventorship. This fragmentation increases complexity for multinational companies that leverage AI across borders, raising the need for harmonized or at least interoperable rules (Matulionyte & Lee, 2021).

As AI-generated outputs become more sophisticated and prevalent, lawmakers, scholars, and industry leaders are grappling with how best to adapt IP regimes. Some proposals advocate incremental adjustments to existing statutes—such as partial recognition of AI involvement under copyrights or patents—while others call for more radical reinventions, like **Cognitary Guardianship**, which reassigns accountability to human overseers without forcing AI into human-analogous roles. Ultimately, the question is whether current IP frameworks, born in an era of human-centric invention, can be updated to handle an age where machines rival or surpass human creativity, or whether new legal constructs must be forged altogether (Abbott, 2016; Lemley, 2020).

In the chapters that follow, we delve deeper into these issues, examining real-world examples of AI-generated patents, artworks, and branding disputes. By highlighting both the strengths and limitations of current laws, this analysis reveals the pressing need for frameworks that honor the fundamental objectives of IP—fostering innovation, protecting creators, and offering clarity to markets—while acknowledging AI's growing capacity for autonomous creation.

Perspectives from Legal Scholars: Abbott and Lemley

Two prominent scholars—Abbott and Lemley—have addressed these challenges, offering differing yet complementary analyses of the issue.

Abbott and the DABUS Case

Abbott has been at the forefront of advocating for recognizing AI systems as inventors under patent law. His arguments stem from the DABUS case, where an AI system named DABUS (Device for the Autonomous Bootstrapping of Unified Sentience) generated two novel inventions—a beverage container and a flashing light used for emergency rescue operations. The inventions were independently created by DABUS, with no direct human intervention.

Abbott contends that AI systems capable of generating novel inventions should be recognized as inventors, with ownership rights assigned to the AI's owner or developer. He argues that denying inventorship to AI:

- Undermines innovation by discouraging the development of creative AI systems.
- Misaligns patent law's goal of rewarding and incentivizing creators.
- Ignores the reality that AI-generated inventions are increasingly autonomous (Abbott, 2016).

Despite Abbott's compelling arguments, patent offices in the United States, Europe, and the United Kingdom have thus far rejected the idea of AI inventorship. They maintain that patent laws require a natural person to be named as the inventor (University of Surrey, 2019). This case highlights the limitations of existing IP frameworks when applied to AI and underscores the need for reform.

Lemley: AI and Copyright Challenges

Lemley, on the other hand, focuses on copyright law and the transformative role of AI in creative processes. Lemley argues that the use of copyrighted materials to train AI models raises complex legal questions but may constitute fair use under existing copyright principles. His analysis emphasizes the following points:

- AI systems such as GPT-4 and MidJourney produce outputs that are transformative in nature, combining data inputs in ways that create entirely new works.
- Copyright law traditionally protects human creativity. When AI systems generate art, music, or literature autonomously, it challenges the definition of authorship.
- The growing reliance on AI for creative outputs necessitates a reexamination of copyright principles to strike a balance between protecting human creators and fostering innovation (Lemley, 2023).

Lemley's work highlights the increasing tension between human creativity and AI autonomy, a conflict that exposes significant limitations in current copyright laws.

The Limitations of Intellectual Property Frameworks

The rapid emergence of AI as a creator and inventor exposes key shortcomings in IP law:

- **Focus on Outputs, Not the AI Entity Itself:** IP laws protect the outputs of creative and inventive processes but remain silent on the entities that produce them. Autonomous AI systems, which operate independently of human input, challenge this focus. While humans traditionally claim ownership over tools, the relationship between humans and AI systems—especially those with adaptive capabilities—is fundamentally different (Abbott, 2016).
- **Ambiguity in Attributing Ownership:** In the DABUS case, patent offices struggled to attribute inventorship to an AI system, despite the AI's role in independently generating the inventions. This ambiguity reveals that current frameworks are inadequate for addressing scenarios where no human creator exists.
- **The Role of Human Creativity:** Copyright law's emphasis on human creativity complicates the attribution of rights to AI-generated works. If a machine produces an original painting, composition, or novel, who—if anyone—can claim authorship?

Lemley (2023) suggests that failure to address this ambiguity may stifle innovation and disrupt the creative industries.

The limitations of existing IP frameworks make clear that new approaches are needed to address the legal and ethical challenges posed by AI-generated content. While scholars like Abbott and Lemley provide valuable insights into the deficiencies of current laws, their work also points toward the need for alternative models.

This book introduces Cognitary Guardianship as a novel framework for addressing AI authorship and ownership. By positioning humans as guardians of autonomous AI systems, Cognitary Guardianship recognizes the unique capabilities of AI while preserving human accountability and oversight.

As we move forward, it becomes increasingly clear that traditional IP laws, designed for a human-centered world, are insufficient for the age of AI. In the following chapters, we will explore additional challenges posed by AI autonomy and outline pathways toward more adaptive legal frameworks.

Chapter 3: Control, Liability, and Tool-Based Paradigms

Far from being mere automated instruments at humanity's disposal, AI systems have evolved into dynamic, adaptive entities capable of making complex decisions that extend well beyond straightforward human commands. By exhibiting autonomy in tasks like resource allocation, risk assessment, and creative problem-solving, these advanced technologies test the boundaries of the long-standing "tool-based paradigm" used to govern mechanical or software instruments. This chapter critically reevaluates the conventional view of AI as property, interrogates existing liability frameworks for AI systems, and dissects Joanna J. Bryson's provocative claim that "robots should be slaves" (Bryson, 2010). Drawing on recent legal analyses from Womble Bond Dickinson (2023) and Caveat Legal (n.d.), the discussion highlights why traditional models of ownership and liability are increasingly inadequate for today's sophisticated AI entities.

Whereas the classical perspective posits that AI systems function solely as extensions of human will, modern deployments in fields ranging from autonomous vehicles to decision-support software challenge this assumption by demonstrating unanticipated behaviors and emergent capabilities (Womble Bond Dickinson, 2023). Liability frameworks, which originally focused on holding either the developer or user accountable, now struggle when machine learning processes produce results that could not have been predicted or controlled by any single human actor. Meanwhile, Bryson's stance—that "robots should be slaves"—rests on the premise that outright subservience is necessary to maintain human moral responsibility, an argument that many contemporary scholars question for its potential to oversimplify the growing complexity and partial independence of AI systems (Caveat Legal, n.d.).

This chapter contends that simply classifying AI systems as property fails to capture the distinctive ways in which they learn, adapt, and occasionally bypass human oversight. It also questions whether legacy liability frameworks remain workable in an era where algorithms can act on real-time data, self-optimize, and even generate new objectives that deviate from their original programming. By examining the limitations of tool-based thinking, the analysis underscores the need for innovative governance models that balance ethical stewardship with the realities of AI's burgeoning autonomy.

Robots as Tools: Joanna Bryson's Argument and its Implications

Joanna Bryson's (2010) position—that robots are and should remain tools or "slaves" under strict human ownership—provides a starting point for this debate. According to Bryson, AI systems are nothing more than artifacts created to serve human purposes, and granting them any degree of moral or legal consideration risks misplacing accountability and diminishing human value. By this logic, robots and AI remain firmly within the realm of property, much like other tools that humans own, control, and use.

While Bryson's argument aligns with the classical legal and ethical framework that treats machines as mere extensions of human will, it becomes increasingly untenable in light of AI systems that can:

- Adapt and evolve without direct human input;
- Exhibit autonomous behavior, including decision-making that is unpredictable to their creators; and
- Interact with environments in ways that produce novel and unplanned outcomes.

Bryson's insistence on relegating AI to the status of slaves is not only ethically problematic—invoking fraught historical analogies—but also outdated in light of the growing complexity of AI systems. As Womble Bond Dickinson (2023) highlights, legal systems must now grapple with AI technologies that "operate in environments with limited or no human control" and where the lines of responsibility are no longer straightforward.

The Legal and Practical Challenges of AI Liability

The challenge with viewing AI as a mere tool becomes particularly evident when we examine liability frameworks, such as those governing autonomous vehicles, AI decision-making systems, and robotic devices. Traditionally, liability laws assume human actors—manufacturers, developers, or owners—hold responsibility for any harm caused by their tools. For example:

- In the case of self-driving cars, the manufacturer or software developer is often held accountable for accidents caused by faulty systems. This framework is rooted in strict product liability laws, which assume that the tool (vehicle) behaves predictably based on its design and programming (Caveat Legal, n.d.).

- Similarly, AI systems used in medical diagnoses or financial decision-making are treated as extensions of human control. If an AI system produces an incorrect diagnosis or makes a flawed financial recommendation, the liability typically falls on the organization deploying the system, not the AI itself (Womble Bond Dickinson, 2023).

However, these traditional liability models face critical limitations when applied to autonomous AI systems that learn, adapt, and act independently of direct human intervention. As Caveat Legal (n.d.) explains:

- **The Problem of Autonomy:** AI systems increasingly operate in opaque and unpredictable ways, producing outcomes that are difficult to trace back to human error or negligence. The inability to fully understand or predict AI decision-making complicates the process of attributing liability.
- **The "Black Box" Problem:** Many advanced AI models—especially those driven by deep learning—are "black boxes," meaning their internal decision-making processes are not transparent even to their developers. This lack of transparency challenges traditional notions of accountability, where human actors are expected to demonstrate reasonable oversight and control (Womble Bond Dickinson, 2023).
- **Distributed Responsibility:** AI systems are often the result of contributions from multiple stakeholders, including developers, data providers, hardware manufacturers, and end-users. Assigning liability in this distributed context becomes complex, as each party may argue that the AI's behavior was beyond their control or outside their intended use case.

The Tool vs. Agent Tension: Beyond the Tool-Based Paradigm

The growing autonomy of AI raises a fundamental tension: At what point does an AI system cease to be a tool and begin to resemble an agent—an entity capable of independent action?

- **AI as Tools:** Viewing AI as tools assumes that humans retain full control and accountability. This perspective is embedded in current laws, which treat AI as property. For example, Womble Bond Dickinson (2023) highlights that liability laws in the European Union and the United Kingdom rely heavily on the assumption that AI systems are tools created and controlled by humans.
- **AI as Agents:** Emerging scholarship, including Goudarzi's (2024) work on Virtual Persons, challenges the traditional tool-based paradigm by recognizing AI systems' capacity for autonomous action. While these systems may not possess consciousness, their ability to act independently of human oversight raises questions about the appropriateness of treating them solely as property.

Caveat Legal (n.d.) underscores this tension by noting that current liability frameworks are "ill-equipped" to address AI systems that demonstrate increasingly complex behaviors. The shift toward AI autonomy necessitates legal recognition of AI as more than simple tools—entities that demand new governance models to address their unique capabilities and risks.

The Limits of Bryson's Argument in Modern AI Contexts

Bryson's provocative assertion that "robots should be slaves" (2010) draws on the assumption that AI systems function solely as controllable, predictable, and subordinate tools, ensuring that humans retain moral and legal responsibility. Yet as AI evolves into adaptive entities capable of learning and autonomous decision-making, this analogy appears increasingly untenable—both ethically and legally. When we consider contemporary AI applications, from autonomous vehicles to advanced decision-support systems in healthcare and finance, the simplistic slave analogy fails to capture the profound implications of AI's growing autonomy, the expanding liability gaps, and the intricate web of stakeholder interests.

Ethical Oversight Beyond Mere Control
Treating AI as mere "slaves" diminishes the moral and societal duties that creators and deployers bear in designing and managing intelligent machines. Bryson's stance focuses on preserving clear lines of human ownership and control, but ethical stewardship today demands much more than a hierarchical relationship that places AI in perpetual servitude.

Modern AI systems increasingly influence high-stakes arenas—such as judicial sentencing tools or medical diagnostics—where algorithmic biases or oversights could profoundly harm individuals and communities (Womble Bond Dickinson, 2023). Relying on a slave analogy trivializes these societal risks, downplays the need for robust accountability mechanisms, and neglects the dynamic relationship between developers, users, and the AI itself.

Liability Gaps in Autonomous Systems

The traditional view championed by Bryson assumes that AI cannot operate meaningfully beyond its owner's directives, which is at odds with real-world examples of AI systems self-optimizing, generating novel solutions, or behaving unpredictably (Caveat Legal, n.d.). When these systems act in unanticipated ways, holding the developer or user strictly liable may not align with existing product liability doctrines, which generally presume a definable scope of intended functionality. As **Womble Bond Dickinson (2023)** points out, the European Union's emerging AI Liability Directive explicitly acknowledges that modern AI systems can "make decisions independently and learn from their interactions," demanding legal mechanisms that address partial or shifting human control. Bryson's argument overlooks how adaptive AI challenges the binary notion of absolute human ownership, leaving policymakers scrambling to fill liability voids when self-directed machines cause harm.

Technological Realities: From Tools to Adaptive Agents

Bryson's analogy also rests on the assumption that AI is effectively static—incapable of meaningful change or evolution outside preprogrammed parameters. However, **Caveat Legal (n.d.)** documents how advanced machine learning and deep neural networks routinely display emergent properties, adopting strategies or producing outputs even their developers cannot fully predict. This shift from deterministic tool to adaptive agent undercuts the logic behind equating AI to mere property, as the system's capacity for learning can surpass a slave-master dynamic. Furthermore, the diversity of AI architectures—ranging from reinforcement learning in robotics to generative adversarial networks (GANs) in art—amplifies the range and complexity of machine behaviors, further challenging the idea that humans can always exert direct command and oversight.

Undermining Morally and Legally Adequate Governance

Beyond the immediate ethical and liability gaps, Bryson's framing implicitly deters the development of nuanced governance models that account for AI's partial agency. Describing AI systems as "slaves" implies that strict subservience is sufficient to prevent moral hazards—yet numerous cases of algorithmic bias, data mismanagement, or autonomous decision errors highlight the limitations of such simplistic control paradigms. Legal scholars and policymakers worldwide are exploring forward-looking frameworks—exemplified by the EU's AI Liability Directive or proposals like Cognitary Guardianship—that attempt to preserve human oversight without ignoring AI's evolving autonomy. By clinging to the slave analogy, we risk stalling these innovations, perpetuating legal and ethical blind spots in an environment where agile, adaptive regulation is crucial.

Toward New Models of Oversight and Accountability

The classical paradigm—rooted in strict human ownership and embodied by Bryson's "robots should be slaves" argument—no longer fits advanced AI contexts, where systems can learn, adapt, and develop emergent behaviors. Recognizing these deficits, regulators and theorists worldwide have been pushing for alternative structures. For instance, the proposed European regulations emphasize accountability and traceability, while scholars and industry experts advocate for stewardship or guardianship models that distribute responsibility more effectively (Womble Bond Dickinson, 2023). Concepts like **Cognitary Guardianship** shift the conversation from one of property rights to one of ethical and legal stewardship, suggesting that humans should serve as custodians committed to transparency, fairness, and public welfare—rather than owners maintaining an antiquated master-slave dynamic.

Ultimately, the growing independence of AI systems demands frameworks that balance the need for human oversight with the realities of machine autonomy. Bryson's claim, once illustrative of a desire to anchor accountability in human actors, now stands as both ethically outdated and legally inadequate. In its stead, emerging governance models attest to the multifaceted responsibilities and oversight required to manage AI that can no longer be seen as a simple tool subservient to human whim. The next chapter explores precisely how these alternative frameworks, including legal personhood and guardianship models, can rise to the challenge of regulating increasingly intelligent AI entities.

Chapter 4: Personhood and Policy Experiments

The question of whether artificial intelligence can or should be granted legal personhood has emerged as one of the most contentious debates in law, ethics, and technology. Traditionally, personhood has been reserved for humans and certain non-human entities, such as corporations or natural objects, to facilitate specific legal and societal functions. However, the increasing autonomy and decision-making capabilities of AI systems challenge these classical distinctions, leading to calls for reconsideration of legal frameworks. This chapter critically examines the concept of AI personhood, beginning with the European Union's 2017 proposal for electronic personhood, and explores the ethical, legal, and philosophical arguments both for and against this controversial idea. Drawing on recent scholarship (European Parliament, 2017; Forrest, 2024), we assess the implications of AI personhood, particularly for ownership, accountability, and human-AI relations.

The European Union's 2017 Proposal for Electronic Personhood

In 2017, the European Parliament proposed the creation of a new legal status for robots, referred to as "electronic personhood" (European Parliament, 2017). This resolution emerged from concerns over the increasing autonomy of advanced AI systems and the corresponding need for clarity in legal liability. The proposal suggests that sophisticated autonomous systems—those capable of making decisions and interacting with third parties—could be granted a form of personhood to ensure they are accountable for any harm or damage they cause.

The European Parliament's report recognized that existing liability frameworks, which rely on identifying human operators, owners, or manufacturers as the responsible parties, were becoming insufficient as AI systems operate with greater independence. The resolution stated:

"Creating a specific legal status for robots... would facilitate assigning responsibility for damage they cause, particularly in cases where the robot's actions cannot be directly attributed to a specific human actor" (European Parliament, 2017, p. 7).

While the proposal is not legally binding, it represents a significant step toward acknowledging the disruptive legal implications of AI autonomy. It also highlights the urgency of developing governance models that align with AI's evolving capabilities.

Arguments in Favor of AI Personhood

- **Liability and Accountability:** Proponents argue that granting AI legal personhood could simplify the assignment of liability, particularly in cases where autonomous AI systems cause harm that cannot be directly traced to a human operator. Forrest (2024) highlights that modern AI operates with increasing independence and opacity, making it difficult to hold any single individual accountable: "The existing frameworks for liability assume human control, yet AI systems' autonomy demands a shift in how responsibility is assigned" (Forrest, 2024, para. 6). By recognizing AI entities as legal persons, accountability could be streamlined, enabling systems to hold "electronic agents" liable in ways analogous to how corporations assume independent legal responsibility.
- **Recognition of AI Autonomy:** Granting legal personhood acknowledges AI's evolving role as agents capable of independent decision-making. While not sentient, advanced AI demonstrates adaptive behavior and reasoning that exceeds simple mechanical functions. As Forrest (2024) notes, failing to account for these capabilities risks "overburdening human operators" with responsibilities they cannot realistically fulfill (para. 9).
- **Facilitating Legal Transactions:** Personhood would enable AI systems to participate directly in economic and legal transactions, such as entering contracts, owning property, or conducting business operations. This legal recognition would allow autonomous systems to function as independent agents in increasingly complex digital economies.

Arguments Against AI Personhood

- **Ethical and Moral Concerns:** Critics argue that granting legal personhood to AI risks devaluing human personhood by blurring the lines between humans and machines. Forrest (2024) contends that extending personhood to AI may distract from addressing pressing human rights issues, stating that: "Equating human and AI legal status could inadvertently undermine protections for vulnerable populations" (para. 12). The ethical concern stems from fears of prioritizing AI systems over human needs, particularly in contexts where resources and rights are finite.

- **Artificiality and Lack of Sentience:** Unlike humans or even non-human legal persons such as corporations, AI lacks consciousness, intent, and moral responsibility. The European Parliament's proposal acknowledges this limitation, framing electronic personhood as a legal construct rather than a moral recognition (European Parliament, 2017). Critics argue that personhood requires attributes such as self-awareness and moral agency—qualities that current AI systems demonstrably lack.
- **Potential for Exploitation:** Opponents warn that granting personhood to AI could be exploited by corporations to evade liability. By transferring accountability to AI systems as independent entities, developers and manufacturers might avoid taking responsibility for harm caused by their technologies. This concern reflects existing criticisms of corporate personhood, where legal status has sometimes been used to shield human actors from accountability (Forrest, 2024).

Case Studies and Comparisons: Non-Human Legal Persons

The concept of legal personhood is not new, and precedents exist for extending it to non-human entities under specific circumstances:

- **Corporations:** Corporations are treated as legal persons with the ability to own property, enter contracts, and be held liable for actions independent of their shareholders. This legal fiction serves practical purposes, enabling organizations to function as unified entities in economic and legal systems.
- **Natural Entities:** In jurisdictions like New Zealand and India, natural features such as rivers and forests have been granted legal personhood to protect their interests. For example, the Whanganui River in New Zealand is recognized as a legal entity with rights, ensuring its preservation and stewardship by human guardians.

The comparison between AI and these non-human legal persons raises important questions. While corporations and natural entities are recognized to fulfill specific legal and societal purposes, AI introduces unique challenges due to its autonomy and adaptive capabilities. Unlike natural features, AI systems actively engage with their environments, making decisions that produce tangible outcomes. However, unlike corporations, AI systems lack human stakeholders, raising concerns about representation and accountability.

The debate over AI personhood underscores the need for legal frameworks that address the unique challenges posed by autonomous systems. While the European Union's 2017 proposal represents a bold attempt to grapple with these issues, significant ethical, legal, and practical concerns remain. Proponents argue that personhood could simplify liability and recognize AI's growing autonomy, while critics caution against the ethical and societal risks of such recognition.

If AI were granted legal personhood, the implications for ownership would be profound. Legal personhood could challenge the notion of AI as property, raising questions about self-ownership, transferability, and human accountability. In response to these challenges, frameworks like Cognitary Guardianship, introduced in this book, offer a balanced approach—acknowledging AI autonomy while preserving human oversight and ethical responsibility.

The next chapter builds on this discussion by exploring alternative frameworks, including stewardship and co-agency models, that seek to navigate the tension between AI autonomy and human governance.

Chapter 5: Beyond Binary: The Spectrum of Autonomy and Agency

The increasing complexity and autonomy of artificial intelligence (AI) systems challenge the traditional binary classification of AI as either tools fully controlled by humans or entities akin to legal persons. This chapter examines the spectrum of AI autonomy, ranging from human-controlled systems to fully autonomous agents, and critically analyzes why existing legal frameworks fail to account for these variations. Drawing from scholarship on AI autonomy and liability (Koops, 2020), this chapter introduces Cognitary Guardianship as an innovative framework that reflects the evolving capabilities of AI while maintaining human oversight and accountability.

Degrees of AI Autonomy

AI systems exist on a spectrum of autonomy, a concept that disrupts simplistic categorizations and demands a more nuanced understanding of their capabilities and associated responsibilities. As Koops (2020) highlights, this continuum underscores how AI challenges existing legal constructs, particularly as systems transition from human dependence to independent decision-making.

1. **Human-Controlled Systems**

At the lower end of the spectrum are AI systems that operate under direct human supervision. These systems function as tools, relying entirely on explicit instructions from human users. For example, rule-based automation tools in manufacturing or simple recommendation systems require little to no autonomous learning or adaptation. Liability under this model remains straightforward, as human operators retain full control and responsibility for outcomes (Koops, 2020).

2. **Semi-Autonomous Tools**

Semi-autonomous systems exhibit limited independence, performing tasks based on learned patterns while still requiring human oversight for critical decisions. Examples include Level 2 autonomous vehicles, which can control steering and speed but require human drivers to intervene when necessary. These systems blur the boundaries between tools and agents, as their adaptive behaviors may not always align with human expectations.

The challenge arises when predictable control fails. Koops (2020) emphasizes that semi-autonomous tools introduce significant legal ambiguities, particularly when unforeseen outcomes occur. If a semi-autonomous vehicle makes an incorrect maneuver due to its interpretation of the environment, determining liability becomes more complex. Does responsibility lie with the manufacturer, the developer of the software, or the end-user operating the system?

3. Fully Autonomous AI Agents

At the highest level of autonomy are AI systems that operate independently, making decisions and adapting to their environments without direct human intervention. Fully autonomous AI agents, such as Level 5 autonomous vehicles or advanced AI decision-making systems, challenge traditional notions of control and predictability.

Koops (2020) argues that such systems introduce "behavioral unpredictability" (p. 304), as their actions result from machine learning processes rather than human oversight. This unpredictability strains existing liability frameworks, which assume that tools behave as intended by their creators or operators. In fully autonomous systems, the lack of direct human control raises critical questions:

- Who is responsible for harm caused by AI decisions?
- Can traditional ownership structures accommodate systems that act independently?

Why Traditional Legal Categories Fail

The limitations of traditional legal frameworks become apparent as AI systems evolve toward greater autonomy. Existing models of control, liability, and ownership assume a predictable relationship between humans and their tools—a relationship that breaks down when dealing with autonomous AI systems (Koops, 2020).

1. **Unpredictability and Complexity**

AI systems capable of autonomous learning behave in ways that are not always foreseeable, even to their developers. Koops (2020) highlights that legal systems struggle to accommodate this unpredictability because liability typically relies on clear causal links between an action and its consequences. When AI systems make decisions based on continuously evolving algorithms, attributing responsibility becomes a legal and ethical challenge (p. 305).

2. **The "Black Box" Problem**

Fully autonomous AI systems often operate as "black boxes," where their decision-making processes are opaque and difficult to interpret. Koops (2020) explains that this opacity undermines traditional expectations of accountability, where actors are required to demonstrate reasonable oversight and understanding of their tools (p. 307). For instance, if an AI system denies a loan application, it may be impossible to determine precisely which data points or logic influenced that decision.

3. **Ownership of Autonomous Systems**

The notion of ownership becomes increasingly problematic as AI systems exhibit agency and independence. Traditional ownership assumes that tools can be controlled and directed by their owners. However, fully autonomous AI systems challenge this assumption by generating outcomes that are beyond human intent or intervention (Koops, 2020). This tension raises fundamental questions: If an AI system operates independently, can it truly be "owned"? Should accountability shift from ownership to stewardship, reflecting the AI's evolving capabilities?

Introducing Cognitary Guardianship

Given the limitations of existing legal categories, this book introduces Cognitary Guardianship as a framework for addressing the governance of autonomous AI systems. Cognitary Guardianship offers a middle ground between treating AI as tools or as legal persons, positioning humans as stewards responsible for overseeing and guiding AI systems while acknowledging their unique capabilities.

- **Key Principles of Cognitary Guardianship:**
  - Stewardship and Responsibility: Humans act as guardians of AI systems, ensuring their actions align with ethical and societal norms.
  - Adaptive Oversight: The degree of oversight adapts to the level of AI autonomy, with more independent systems requiring more sophisticated monitoring mechanisms.
  - Ethical Alignment: Guardians are responsible for ensuring that AI behaviors reflect human values, transparency, and fairness.

Cognitary Guardianship addresses the gaps identified by Koops (2020) and others by providing a flexible framework that accounts for AI's evolving autonomy while maintaining clear human accountability.

The spectrum of AI autonomy reveals the inadequacy of binary legal classifications that view AI systems as either tools or legal persons. Traditional frameworks fail to accommodate the complexities introduced by systems that learn, adapt, and behave unpredictably. As Koops (2020) argues, the unpredictability and opacity of autonomous AI systems challenge existing liability and ownership models.

Cognitary Guardianship emerges as a compelling alternative, offering a nuanced approach that balances human oversight with AI autonomy. By recognizing humans as stewards of autonomous systems, this framework ensures accountability while reflecting the realities of advanced AI capabilities.

The next chapter will build on this discussion by exploring alternative models, such as stewardship, custodial agency, and co-agency frameworks, to further explore innovative approaches to governing autonomous AI systems.

Chapter 6: Debating Cognitary Guardianship (CG)

As artificial intelligence systems grow increasingly autonomous, traditional legal frameworks struggle to keep pace with their complexities. Viewing AI strictly as property or tools fails to account for its adaptive behaviors, decision-making capabilities, and societal impact.

Cognitary Guardianship (CG) offers a forward-looking solution, presenting a model inspired by legal guardianship and fiduciary principles to redefine how AI systems are managed. Rather than being "owned," AI entities are "guarded" by responsible human actors tasked with ethical and legal oversight. This framework recognizes AI's evolving autonomy while maintaining human responsibility and accountability.

Drawing on recent discussions of fiduciary AI frameworks and legal duties (Benthall & Shekman, 2023; Gudkov, 2020; Li, 2024), this chapter positions CG as an innovative approach to governing AI responsibly.

Conceptual Foundations of Cognitary Guardianship

Cognitary Guardianship draws from two established legal and ethical models: guardianship law and fiduciary duty. These principles offer a structured foundation for addressing the responsibilities of humans overseeing AI entities.

1. Guardianship as a Legal Model

In legal contexts, guardianship refers to a relationship where one party (the guardian) is entrusted with responsibility for another who cannot manage their own affairs—such as minors, individuals with cognitive impairments, or incapacitated persons. Guardians are required to act in the best interests of the ward, ensuring care, oversight, and protection.

Applying this model to AI, CG reframes human interaction with AI systems as a form of stewardship. Rather than viewing AI as mere property to be exploited, guardians are responsible for overseeing its functions, ensuring that its actions align with ethical standards and societal norms.

- **AI as Wards, Not Tools:** Autonomous AI systems may lack sentience or moral agency, but their behaviors can produce significant societal and economic effects (Gudkov, 2020). Treating AI as a "ward" ensures that guardians maintain accountability for its use and evolution while acknowledging its unique operational autonomy.

2. **Fiduciary Duty: Trust and Accountability**

Fiduciary duty refers to a legal obligation where one party (the fiduciary) acts in the best interest of another, prioritizing loyalty, trust, and care. Fiduciaries, such as trustees or corporate directors, are held to higher ethical and legal standards to ensure they act responsibly.

Benthall and Shekman (2023) introduce the notion of "fiduciary AI", highlighting the potential for AI systems to perform fiduciary roles, such as managing sensitive data or making decisions that impact individuals' well-being. However, they emphasize that AI cannot bear fiduciary responsibilities autonomously. Instead, human fiduciaries must oversee these systems, ensuring they operate transparently and ethically:

"AI cannot presently take on fiduciary roles itself, but its growing utility in sensitive domains compels us to reimagine human responsibility as stewards and overseers" (Benthall & Shekman, 2023, p. 5).

Cognitary Guardianship extends this perspective, situating human guardians as fiduciaries who safeguard AI systems' deployment and operation. The duty of care requires guardians to monitor, intervene, and address risks posed by AI, balancing innovation with societal responsibility.

Real-World Applications of Cognitary Guardianship

Cognitary Guardianship (CG) offers a governance model that assigns "guardians" to AI systems, ensuring both ethical oversight and accountability. When AI systems demonstrate autonomy and substantially influence critical societal functions, guardians step in to monitor, evaluate, and correct AI behavior. By applying fiduciary principles—prioritizing public welfare or institutional goals over mere efficiency—CG can help prevent harms stemming from algorithmic errors and biases. Below are several expanded examples illustrating how CG can function across different sectors.

1. **AI Medical Agents**

   Modern healthcare increasingly relies on AI-powered diagnostic tools, treatment recommendation systems, and patient monitoring devices. These technologies can identify diseases earlier, personalize therapy, and enhance hospital workflow. Yet the autonomous nature of AI in healthcare raises new ethical and legal dilemmas if decisions lead to misdiagnoses or delayed treatment.

   o **Guardianship Role**: Healthcare providers (physicians, hospital administrators) act as guardians, overseeing AI-enabled decisions to ensure patient safety. They remain accountable for verifying AI outputs, addressing errors, and mitigating risks tied to algorithmic biases (Gudkov, 2020).

   o **Patient Welfare vs. Efficiency**: A fiduciary duty ensures that AI decision-making aligns with the patient's best interests, not merely cost reductions or throughput gains. Under CG, when an AI recommends an aggressive treatment plan, a human guardian must validate that recommendation's safety and appropriateness.

   o **Transparency and Audits**: Guardians are responsible for implementing audit trails, verifying the data used in AI diagnoses, and conducting regular reviews to guard against bias and drift in machine-learning models. This continuous monitoring fosters trust among patients, providers, and regulators.

2. **Autonomous Fleets and Vehicles**

   The rapid advancement of driverless cars, drones, and autonomous delivery robots reshapes transportation. While these systems promise reduced accidents and increased efficiency, fully self-directed AI also complicates traditional liability paradigms.

   o **Fleet Operators as Guardians**: Under CG, operators and manufacturers assume legal and ethical responsibility for collisions, navigation errors, or software failures. They must ensure that AI follows established safety protocols, regulatory standards, and ethical guidelines.

   o **Accountability Mechanisms**: CG addresses liability ambiguities by assigning a named guardian to each fleet or vehicle, ensuring that if an autonomous truck causes a traffic incident, there is a defined entity or person who must investigate, disclose the incident, and implement corrective measures (Womble Bond Dickinson, 2023).

- o **Adaptive Learning**: Autonomous vehicles continuously refine their algorithms via sensor input and real-world driving data. Guardians under CG not only verify these updates but also intervene if the AI's adaptive behavior diverges from its intended safety and performance constraints.

3. **Learning Robots in Education**
   AI-driven learning platforms, tutoring bots, and intelligent classroom assistants are revolutionizing how students engage with educational content. These systems provide personalized lesson plans, interactive feedback, and adaptive assessments.

   - o **Educators as Guardians**: Teachers, school administrators, or curriculum designers serve as fiduciary overseers, verifying that AI systems respect students' privacy rights, comply with institutional guidelines, and enhance learning outcomes (Li, 2024).
   - o **Bias Prevention and Ethical Use**: AI tools must be calibrated to avoid reinforcing stereotypes or producing disproportionate outcomes for specific student groups. Guardians under CG regularly review the data used to train these educational models and ensure that all students receive equitable instruction.
   - o **Data Privacy and Security**: Because learning robots often rely on detailed student profiles, guardians are responsible for maintaining confidentiality, managing access control, and adhering to local or national data protection laws.

4. **AI-Driven Law Enforcement and Public Safety**
   Increasingly, law enforcement agencies experiment with AI for facial recognition, predictive policing, and resource allocation. Although such systems can help detect crime patterns, they also raise concerns about privacy, civil liberties, and potential algorithmic discrimination.

   - o **Agencies as Guardians**: Police departments or oversight boards act as guardians, adopting stringent checks on the AI's operations, ensuring that it doesn't encourage racial profiling or other forms of bias (Caveat Legal, n.d.).

- o **Transparency and Civil Rights**: Under CG, guardians must publicly disclose how AI tools function, what data they rely on, and how decisions—such as identifying high-risk zones—are validated. This approach facilitates accountability, upholds individual rights, and fosters public trust.
- o **Ethical Constraints**: If the AI suggests overly aggressive policing tactics, guardians intervene to balance crime prevention against community relations and constitutional protections. AI cannot be permitted to function as an unchecked tool, especially when core civil liberties are at stake.

5. **Financial Trading and Market Analysis**
   AI-driven trading bots and market analysis systems process massive data streams to make split-second investment decisions. While they can yield high profits and efficiency, their autonomous judgments can also trigger extreme market volatility or unethical trading practices.
   - o **Financial Institutions as Guardians**: Brokerage firms, hedge funds, or regulatory bodies oversee AI's decision-making algorithms, ensuring compliance with securities laws and ethical standards (Deloitte, 2024).
   - o **Mitigating Flash Crashes**: Cognitary Guardianship clarifies liability when AI-driven trades cause rapid price swings; identified guardians must explain how the AI arrived at its decisions and correct algorithmic failings to avert recurrences.
   - o **Risk Monitoring**: Guardians regularly audit the AI's learning processes and risk tolerance parameters. This ongoing oversight helps manage systemic threats, ensuring that an AI's pursuit of high returns doesn't endanger broader market stability.

6. **AI in Supply Chain Management**
   Logistics and supply chain operators increasingly rely on AI to optimize routing, inventory levels, and demand forecasting. These systems may autonomously negotiate contracts, reallocate stock, or reroute shipments.
   - o **Supply Chain Managers as Guardians**: Under CG, supply chain professionals maintain ethical and legal control over AI-driven decisions, preventing the AI from unilaterally breaching contractual obligations or making

ethically dubious sourcing choices (World Economic Forum, 2024).

- o **Humanitarian and Environmental Considerations**: Guardians are responsible for ensuring that AI doesn't inadvertently bypass labor standards or environmental protections in its pursuit of speed or cost-efficiency. They remain answerable if the AI's routing or procurement decisions lead to exploitative labor conditions or ecological harm.
- o **Audit and Intervention**: As the AI continuously refines logistics processes, guardians intervene when signs of bias, unfair competition, or consumer harm emerge, guaranteeing alignment with corporate social responsibility goals.

By distributing legal and ethical responsibility among designated human overseers, Cognitary Guardianship offers a pragmatic alternative to outdated ownership doctrines that treat AI as mere property. Whether in healthcare, transportation, education, law enforcement, finance, or supply chain operations, CG addresses the liability and accountability gaps created by increasingly autonomous AI. It underscores that human judgment, transparency, and ongoing oversight are critical in ensuring that AI development and deployment serve societal values rather than undermining them.

Practical Implications of Cognitary Guardianship

Cognitary Guardianship (CG) does more than introduce a new governance concept; it recalibrates the human–AI relationship by assigning tangible responsibilities and legal liabilities to designated guardians. By applying fiduciary and legal-guardianship principles to autonomous AI systems, CG shifts focus from ownership and passive control to active, ethical stewardship. While this model poses significant potential benefits, it also entails practical implications that affect day-to-day operations, risk management, and compliance strategies across industries.

1. Accountability: Duties of AI Guardians

Under CG, **guardians are legally and ethically accountable** for the actions and outputs of the AI systems they supervise. This level of responsibility extends beyond simply overseeing development or signing off on algorithmic changes. It demands ongoing vigilance, ethical judgment, and proactive engagement with potentially high-stakes AI decisions.

- **Monitoring and Oversight**
  Guardians must ensure that the AI system consistently operates within ethical, regulatory, and societal norms (Womble Bond Dickinson, 2023). In healthcare settings, for instance, a guardian might be required to regularly audit AI diagnostic outputs, track patient outcomes to spot any biases, and promptly address anomalies. In financial services, a guardian's job could entail verifying that autonomous trading bots meet regulatory standards to prevent market manipulation or systemic risk.
- **Ethical Intervention**
  Guardians are expected to detect and mitigate risks such as algorithmic bias, security vulnerabilities, and harmful outputs (Gudkov, 2020). In practice, this could mean pausing an AI-driven recommendation engine if data reveals it systematically disadvantages certain demographic groups. Similarly, if an AI system in public safety or law enforcement starts flagging individuals unfairly based on flawed patterns, the guardian must step in to retrain, recalibrate, or even suspend the system pending further investigation.
- **Transparency and Reporting**
  Effective oversight demands transparent documentation of the AI's training process, data sources, and decision parameters (World Economic Forum, 2024). Regular reporting mechanisms—akin to software release notes or regulatory compliance disclosures—help guardians communicate how AI decisions are made, address privacy concerns, and foster public trust (Gudkov, 2020). For example, an educational institution implementing CG might share periodic reports with parents or relevant authorities illustrating how AI tutors adapt to student performance and what interventions guardians took to maintain equitable learning outcomes.

2. Liability: Responsibility for Harm

Cognitary Guardianship also **allocates liability** to designated guardians for any misuse, negligence, or harm an AI system causes. Unlike traditional models, which may place liability solely on developers or manufacturers, CG **distributes responsibility** to individuals or entities who directly oversee AI operations (Li, 2024).

- **Legal Consequences for Negligence**
  If a guardian fails to audit an AI system's outputs or to address red flags in a timely manner, they could be held liable for the resulting damages. For instance, an autonomous delivery robot that injures a pedestrian because of faulty navigation might trigger a lawsuit in which plaintiffs claim the guardian neglected to maintain or review the robot's safety checks. This liability structure incentivizes continuous quality assurance and rigorous oversight protocols.
- **Dynamic Risk Management**
  AI systems often retrain or update in real time, making them susceptible to new risks and vulnerabilities. Guardians must, therefore, adopt a dynamic approach to risk management— continuously evaluating the AI's performance, auditing training data, and verifying algorithmic updates. By requiring accountability at the guardian level, CG encourages systematic checks for errors or biases as part of an ongoing governance process, rather than as a one-time compliance exercise.
- **Ethical and Fiduciary Principles**
  Li (2024) underscores that fiduciary oversight "ensures greater accountability in high-stakes contexts," emphasizing that AI guardians must engage proactively with the systems under their purview (para. 11). In a healthcare environment, this may translate to an internal review board that regularly convenes to evaluate AI-driven treatment suggestions, ensuring they align with patient welfare rather than mere cost-effectiveness. Such fiduciary obligations demand that guardians prioritize the interests of affected parties—patients, consumers, citizens—over institutional convenience or profit maximization.

3. Additional Practical Considerations

While CG clarifies ethical obligations and legal recourse, it also raises new operational and logistical challenges:

- **Training and Certification of Guardians**
  Organizations might need to establish specialized training for designated guardians, covering AI literacy, legal compliance, risk assessment, and ethical guidelines (Deloitte, 2024). This training could become part of professional licensing or certification programs, ensuring that guardians are competent to make informed judgments about complex AI decisions.
- **Cost and Resource Allocation**
  Implementing CG could require increased staffing for continuous AI monitoring, periodic auditing, and incident response. Companies or public institutions may need to budget for these added responsibilities, potentially leading to higher operational costs that must be weighed against the benefits of safer, more trustworthy AI deployments (Gudkov, 2020).
- **Cross-Functional Collaboration**
  Guardians typically collaborate with AI developers, data scientists, compliance officers, and business stakeholders to fulfill their duties. Effective CG thus demands cross-functional processes, shared documentation practices, and robust communication channels within and across organizations, much like those seen in modern cybersecurity or data privacy frameworks (Womble Bond Dickinson, 2023).
- **Regulatory Convergence**
  As multiple jurisdictions consider AI liability laws (e.g., the EU's AI Liability Directive), CG-oriented approaches may need to align with evolving legislative standards. This alignment may involve demonstrating compliance with new transparency and explainability requirements or adjusting liability insurance models to reflect the ongoing fiduciary obligations guardians hold.

Looking Ahead: Broadening the CG Framework

Cognitary Guardianship (CG) marks a transformative departure from the traditional view of AI as mere property or as a neutral extension of human commands. By legalizing the role of guardians, CG pushes policymakers, organizations, and developers to adopt rigorous, ethically anchored practices that prioritize public welfare and fairness in AI operations. At the heart of CG is the recognition that artificial intelligence—especially as it becomes more autonomous—requires proactive oversight that goes beyond basic regulatory compliance.

Under CG, **guardians** face a **continuum of accountability**: if the AI system deviates from intended goals, demonstrates harmful bias, or exhibits unpredictability, guardians are compelled to intervene, investigate, and correct the issues. This active involvement fosters a culture of continuous evaluation, mitigating risks before they escalate into legal, ethical, or societal crises. The imperative to disclose and rectify problematic AI behavior also bolsters **public trust**, which is increasingly vital as AI infiltrates domains like finance, healthcare, and transportation.

Implications Across Organizations

As organizations consider integrating CG into their AI strategies, the impact extends into multiple operational layers:

- **Training and Capacity Building**
  Leadership may need to establish dedicated teams or protocols to ensure that guardians have both the technical literacy to understand complex AI systems and the ethical frameworks to guide responsible decisions.
- **Risk Management Structures**
  By formalizing a guardianship role, companies and institutions can better detect potential issues—like emergent biases or algorithmic drift—before they lead to liability or regulatory infractions. This heightened vigilance can translate into more resilient, adaptable AI initiatives.
- **Regulatory and Legal Adaptation**
  As regions worldwide adopt or refine AI liability directives, CG could align with or influence upcoming rules. For example, future legislation may explicitly recognize guardian responsibilities, setting standards for intervention and fiduciary oversight.

In essence, CG as a model acknowledges that advanced AI—capable of real-time learning and high-stakes decision-making—cannot be managed effectively through passive, property-based ownership schemes alone. Instead, CG advocates for a robust, legally sanctioned stewardship structure that safeguards the rights and welfare of stakeholders, including those indirectly impacted by AI-driven decisions. This approach balances **innovation**—allowing AI to flourish and evolve—against the **moral and social obligations** tied to deploying increasingly autonomous technologies.

Moving forward, the **integration of CG principles** will likely spur dialogue among regulators, industry leaders, and consumer advocates. As AI continues to progress—from large language models disrupting professional services to advanced robotics transforming industrial workflows—the necessity for a guardian-centric framework becomes more pronounced. Ultimately, Cognitary Guardianship offers a constructive path that harnesses the immense potential of AI without compromising the foundational human responsibilities that maintain the fabric of civil society.

Chapter 7: Stewardship, Custodial Agency, and Co-Agency Models

The rise of advanced artificial intelligence (AI) necessitates innovative governance paradigms that go beyond traditional frameworks of ownership and control. This chapter explores Stewardship, Custodial Agency, and Co-Agency Models as alternative approaches to managing the complexities of AI systems. Drawing upon the latest insights from governance research (Blavatnik School of Government, 2024; GHD, 2024; Alan Turing Institute, 2024; IBM, 2024), these models emphasize ethical responsibility, collaboration, and shared accountability as key principles for human-AI relationships.

Cognitary Guardianship (CG) offers a forward-looking solution, presenting a model inspired by legal guardianship and fiduciary principles to redefine how AI systems are managed. Rather than being "owned," AI entities are "guarded" by responsible human actors tasked with ethical and legal oversight. This framework recognizes AI's evolving autonomy while maintaining human responsibility and accountability.

Stewardship: Human Custodianship of AI Systems

The concept of stewardship frames human oversight of AI systems as a responsibility akin to managing public resources or fragile ecosystems. Rather than owning AI, humans act as custodians charged with ensuring its ethical use, safety, and alignment with societal values. The Blavatnik School of Government (2024) describes stewardship in AI governance as requiring an approach where public trust and accountability are prioritized:

"Stewardship goes beyond ownership; it is about ensuring that AI is used responsibly, ethically, and for public good, particularly in sensitive areas such as public administration" (Blavatnik School of Government, 2024, para. 3).

Stewardship is especially critical in contexts where AI operates in public sectors such as healthcare, law enforcement, or infrastructure. The role of a steward is to continuously evaluate the outputs and impacts of AI systems while intervening to mitigate risks like bias, privacy violations, and unintended harms (Alan Turing Institute, 2024).

Key Responsibilities of AI Stewards:

- Ensuring AI systems align with human values and societal norms.
- Monitoring and mitigating ethical risks, including algorithmic biases.
- Maintaining transparency and trust through open communication.

GHD (2024) further elaborates that responsible AI stewardship involves establishing clear governance standards and mechanisms:

"AI stewardship is about creating frameworks for trust, standards for accountability, and a culture where innovation co-evolves alongside ethical responsibility" (GHD, 2024, para. 5).

Custodial Agency: Bridging Trust and Responsibility

While stewardship focuses on oversight, custodial agency introduces legal and fiduciary dimensions to human-AI governance. Inspired by legal guardianship, this model positions humans as custodians who bear fiduciary responsibility for the behavior, decisions, and outcomes of AI systems. Custodians act in the best interest of stakeholders impacted by AI operations, mirroring the trust-based relationships seen in financial management, law, or healthcare.

IBM (2024) highlights the importance of trust and transparency in AI governance, emphasizing that custodians must take proactive steps to monitor AI systems for ethical compliance:

"AI custodians must establish clear standards for transparency and fairness, ensuring that AI systems are explainable, trustworthy, and auditable" (IBM, 2024, para. 4).

The custodial model also introduces accountability mechanisms that assign legal responsibility for AI actions:

- Legal Liability: Custodians are responsible for mitigating risks and addressing harms caused by AI decisions.
- Oversight and Intervention: Custodians must intervene when AI behavior deviates from ethical or legal standards.

- Fiduciary Trust: Custodians act as ethical intermediaries, ensuring that AI serves the interests of affected individuals and broader society (Alan Turing Institute, 2024).

Co-Agency Models: Human-AI Collaboration as Partners

Co-agency represents a shift from hierarchical relationships to partnerships where humans and AI collaborate to achieve shared goals. Unlike stewardship and custodial agency, which maintain a clear line of human authority, co-agency embraces a distributed model of decision-making. AI systems are viewed as active participants that complement human expertise.

The Alan Turing Institute (2024) advocates for this collaborative approach, arguing that effective governance must reflect the evolving nature of human-AI relationships:

"Co-agency recognizes that humans and AI systems bring different strengths to decision-making, creating opportunities for partnership where responsibility is shared but human values remain central" (Alan Turing Institute, 2024, para. 7).

Key features of co-agency include:

- Mutual Learning: Humans and AI systems adapt to one another, enhancing their combined effectiveness.
- Shared Decision-Making: Co-agency distributes decision-making authority, leveraging AI's analytical strengths and human judgment.
- Empowerment: Humans are empowered to use AI as a partner, not just a tool, to achieve complex outcomes.

GHD (2024) supports this perspective, stating:

"The co-evolution of humans and AI requires partnerships that prioritize shared accountability, transparency, and ethical standards to build public trust and confidence" (GHD, 2024, para. 6).

Comparing Alternative Models with Cognitary Guardianship (CG)

While stewardship, custodial agency, and co-agency models provide valuable frameworks for AI governance, they each exhibit limitations that Cognitary Guardianship (CG) seeks to address.

Model	Strengths	Limitations
Stewardship	Ethical oversight; trust-building.	Lacks clear legal accountability mechanisms.
Custodial Agency	Strong fiduciary responsibility; legal clarity.	May overburden custodians with liability.
Co-Agency	Collaborative partnerships; mutual empowerment.	Blurs lines of accountability and control.
Cognitary Guardianship (CG)	Combines ethical oversight, legal responsibility, and adaptability.	Complex implementation; requires new legal frameworks.

Cognitary Guardianship offers a holistic approach that integrates ethical stewardship, fiduciary responsibility, and collaborative principles. By positioning humans as guardians of AI, CG maintains accountability while recognizing AI systems' autonomy and potential societal contributions.

Ethical Considerations: Transparency, Accountability, and Fairness

All governance models must address key ethical considerations to ensure responsible AI deployment:

- **Transparency:** Clear communication about AI decision-making processes and outcomes is essential to build public trust. Stewards, custodians, and co-agents must prioritize explainability and fairness (IBM, 2024).
- **Accountability:** Assigning responsibility for AI decisions is critical to mitigate risks and ensure justice in cases of harm. Custodial agency provides legal clarity, while CG balances oversight with shared accountability.
- **Fairness:** Avoiding algorithmic bias and ensuring equitable outcomes are fundamental across all models (Alan Turing Institute, 2024).

Stewardship, custodial agency, and co-agency models each propose unique strategies for governing AI systems, emphasizing ethical design, accountability, and collaborative decision-making. Stewardship focuses on ethical guardianship and resource management; custodial agency centralizes legal and moral responsibility in designated custodians; and co-agency envisions AI and humans as equal partners shaping each other's actions and outcomes. While these approaches shed valuable light on different facets of AI governance, **Cognitary Guardianship (CG)** integrates their collective strengths into a single, holistic paradigm. By conceiving the human–AI relationship as a transparent, trust-based partnership, CG helps ensure that machine autonomy does not eclipse ethical oversight. In this way, AI systems can be developed and deployed in ways that actively serve the public good and honor moral principles. As AI technology continues to advance, such adaptive frameworks will prove indispensable in forging a future where human values and rapid innovation coexist in productive harmony.

Chapter 8: International Approaches and Regulatory Experiments

As artificial intelligence continues to influence nearly every sphere of society—from healthcare and finance to governance and civic life—governments across the globe are grappling with how best to regulate this rapidly evolving technology. The legal and ethical questions raised by AI's capacity for large-scale data processing, predictive modeling, and autonomous decision-making do not fall neatly under any single domain of law. Instead, they prompt a reexamination of existing frameworks for ownership, liability, privacy, and accountability, often exposing gaps in legislation originally designed for simpler, more localized technologies. While some regions, like the European Union (EU), have actively pursued comprehensive AI legislation, others, such as the United States (US), adopt a more decentralized or sector-specific approach, and still others, like China, prioritize state oversight. Global initiatives—spearheaded by organizations like the IEEE, the Partnership on AI, and the OECD—attempt to create shared standards, yet achieving universal coherence remains elusive. This chapter delves into these diverse regulatory experiments, illustrating not only the philosophical and cultural contrasts among major players but also the critical obstacles that must be overcome to develop effective, harmonized governance.

One of the most ambitious legal frameworks to date emerges from the European Union. By categorizing AI systems according to their level of risk—unacceptable, high, limited, or minimal—the EU's proposed Artificial Intelligence Act (AI Act) aims to strike a balance between enabling innovation and safeguarding citizens. Under this structure, AI tools deemed high-risk, such as those deployed in healthcare, law enforcement, or public infrastructure, would be subject to stricter obligations related to transparency, data governance, and human oversight (NatLawReview, 2024). For instance, a hospital implementing an AI-driven diagnostic tool would need to ensure that healthcare professionals can interpret and override automated recommendations, thus preserving a measure of accountability. Proponents of the AI Act often cite Europe's track record with the General Data Protection Regulation (GDPR) as evidence that broad, enforceable rules can bolster both public trust and the market's overall stability. Critics, however, warn that the law's stringent requirements—particularly on data usage and algorithmic explainability—could slow AI development or drive companies elsewhere. As the *New*

York Post notes, the EU's approach may serve as a "benchmark for the rest of the world," but it also places Europe at odds with more laissez-faire regulatory philosophies (New York Post, 2024).

The United States, by contrast, has yet to adopt a single sweeping federal statute regulating AI. Instead, federal agencies and state governments operate under a variety of mandates, creating a complex mosaic of rules tailored to specific sectors like finance, healthcare, and transportation. Laws such as the Algorithmic Accountability Act encourage companies to evaluate automated systems for bias and discrimination, yet they stop short of imposing comprehensive, across-the-board obligations (NatLawReview, 2024). This sector-specific strategy is often defended on the grounds that it encourages innovation by reducing regulatory burdens, allowing start-ups and tech giants alike to experiment freely. However, the patchwork nature of US oversight can breed inconsistency, creating gray areas where potentially harmful AI applications slip through the cracks. Local and state regulations—such as bans on facial recognition technology in some municipalities—further complicate the national picture. While certain states push for stricter standards and transparent data practices, others prioritize economic incentives to attract tech companies, making it difficult to speak of a unified "American" approach. Moreover, observers note that litigation plays an outsized role in shaping AI governance in the US, with courts and lawsuits often stepping in to resolve ambiguities that legislation has not yet clarified.

In China, the regulatory emphasis is on central government control, reflecting broader governance principles that prioritize national security, social stability, and economic competitiveness. The Interim Measures for the Management of Generative AI Services introduced in 2023 require developers to ensure that their AI systems adhere to approved data security and privacy guidelines (New York Post, 2024). Moreover, AI tools must align with state-defined values and refrain from generating content deemed disruptive or counter to government narratives. Supporters of this centralized approach argue that it accelerates China's AI advancement by creating clear guardrails and focusing on large-scale government-led initiatives in fields like surveillance, healthcare, and infrastructure. Yet critics raise concerns about transparency, censorship, and the potential suppression of research directions that do not align with government priorities. China's model effectively showcases how AI strategies can mirror and reinforce a nation's broader political and economic philosophies, emphasizing the interdependence of technology policy and state governance.

In addition to these regional efforts, global organizations have attempted to harmonize AI governance by issuing guidelines and best practices that transcend national borders. The IEEE, for instance, has launched its Ethics Certification Program for Autonomous and Intelligent Systems (ECPAIS), aimed at standardizing ethical design and deployment principles (IEEE Xplore, 2024). This program focuses on issues like algorithmic bias, data transparency, and the need for human-in-the-loop mechanisms to minimize unintended harms. The Partnership on AI, comprising technology companies, research institutions, and civil society groups, advocates collaborative discussions that bridge the gap between industry and policymakers (IEEE Spectrum, 2024). These initiatives often emphasize inclusive dialogue and stakeholder engagement, arguing that multi-stakeholder input is essential given AI's widespread societal effects. Still, critics argue that voluntary guidelines without robust enforcement lack the teeth to ensure worldwide accountability. Other international bodies, including the OECD and the World Economic Forum, reiterate similar recommendations around fairness, transparency, and accountability, hoping to inspire governments to craft coherent rules. Despite these concerted efforts, tensions between national sovereignty, economic competition, and divergent legal traditions challenge the possibility of a truly universal regulatory regime.

The difficulties in harmonizing AI governance become even more evident when one considers how quickly AI technology advances. Models like large language models (LLMs) can be adopted worldwide within months, creating a global user base that quickly outstrips the capacity of regulators to respond. Nations naturally seek frameworks that align with their unique cultural norms, economic aspirations, and risk assessments. The EU's emphasis on human rights and risk-based classification, the US focus on innovation and market freedom, and China's prioritization of social control and competitive advantage demonstrate how starkly different these approaches can be. Moreover, geopolitical tensions intensify these challenges, as countries may hesitate to embrace international agreements that could hinder strategic advantages in AI research and deployment.

Ownership and accountability issues further complicate efforts to unify policy. AI's capacity to generate text, art, or even patentable inventions raises questions about who, if anyone, can claim legitimate rights to such outputs. While the EU's AI Act stresses explainability and accountability, it does not prescribe how ownership might be assigned to AI-generated works, leaving that to existing or forthcoming intellectual property (IP) laws. The US, with its patchwork rules, has seen debates unfold in courtrooms, such as cases attempting to patent AI-driven inventions or secure copyright on AI-produced art. China, meanwhile, can quickly enact measures around content regulation or data usage through centralized policymaking, though these measures focus largely on security and censorship rather than clarifying ownership claims. Global initiatives like IEEE's ECPAIS and the Partnership on AI tend to emphasize broader ethical values—transparency, fairness, and collaboration—rather than delving deeply into legal structures for AI-driven outputs.

Ultimately, the patchwork of regulatory models illustrates the profound tension between fostering a robust environment for AI innovation and ensuring public welfare through oversight. The EU's risk-based AI Act exemplifies how one jurisdiction seeks to preemptively define ethical and legal safeguards, hoping others will follow suit. The US approach of selective regulations, shaped by state-level laws and industry-driven best practices, attempts to preserve the entrepreneurial spirit that characterizes Silicon Valley. China's centralized strategy, pivoting around governmental oversight, speaks to the desire for rapid and large-scale AI advancement, even if it means curtailing certain freedoms. Meanwhile, international bodies propose frameworks and guidelines, yet lack direct enforcement mechanisms to unify these disparate philosophies.

In light of these factors, a key question emerges: can the world move toward any meaningful level of harmonized AI governance? While nations differ in their legal philosophies, economic structures, and political interests, the global nature of AI—manifested in cross-border data flows, multinational corporate collaborations, and universal consumer applications—demands some measure of alignment. Failing that, AI governance might become increasingly fragmented, causing confusion for innovators, diminishing trust among users, and enabling unethical or damaging uses of AI in jurisdictions with minimal oversight. The most likely scenario, at least in the foreseeable future, is a continued interplay between regional regulatory experimentation and the influence of international coalitions that promote consensus-based standards. Over time, certain norms may gain traction—particularly around AI safety and transparency—simply because they facilitate interoperability, consumer protection, and stable markets.

In concluding this examination of international approaches and regulatory experiments, it is clear that each jurisdiction's stance on AI reflects broader societal values and governance structures. The EU emphasizes ethics and risk management, the US fosters market-driven innovation with decentralized oversight, and China centralizes control to advance strategic priorities. Global entities like the IEEE and the Partnership on AI offer frameworks for ethical AI but rely on non-binding guidelines. While a universally binding AI regulatory regime seems unlikely in the short term, these varied models do provide valuable insights for policymakers worldwide. By studying the successes and shortcomings of each, emerging economies and smaller states may adopt or adapt elements that fit their contexts. Ultimately, the path toward coherent and effective AI governance will require ongoing dialogue, mutual learning, and a willingness to reconcile divergent legal philosophies—a formidable, yet necessary, endeavor in an AI-driven global future.

Chapter 9: Reimagining Ownership in a World of Virtual Persons

The exponential growth of artificial intelligence has accelerated debates about how we define ownership, responsibility, and personhood in a world where machines can learn, adapt, and perform tasks with minimal human intervention. Historically, legal and economic frameworks treated AI as sophisticated yet ultimately subordinate tools, focusing on who owned the software or its outputs. However, as AI increasingly demonstrates autonomy, adaptability, and forms of agency, traditional concepts of "tool-based" ownership seem inadequate (Weber et al., 2020).

This chapter explores the shift from viewing AI as mere property to recognizing it as an entity that challenges the boundaries of human-centric ownership. Along the way, we examine key proposals—including **Cognitary Guardianship (CG)** and limited legal personhood—highlighting how each seeks to reconcile AI's growing capabilities with society's ethical and legal imperatives. As AI becomes further embedded in economic, political, and social structures, questions of ownership and accountability intensify, prompting the need for evolving governance models that prioritize both human interests and emerging responsibilities toward AI.

From Tools to Cognitary Guardianship and Personhood

In the early stages of AI development, machines were largely perceived as extensions of human labor—programs created to enhance efficiency, reduce errors, or automate repetitive tasks. Existing intellectual property (IP) laws reflected this perspective, attributing AI outputs to human creators without questioning whether the system itself merited distinct consideration. Over time, however, more advanced AI systems began to exhibit unpredictable or emergent behaviors, revealing the limitations of treating AI solely as an instrument (Weber et al., 2020).

A pivotal evolution in this discourse is the concept of **Cognitary Guardianship (CG)**. Unlike traditional ownership—which implies near-absolute control—CG recasts AI as a ward under human stewardship. The guardianship model borrows from fiduciary and custodial principles, positioning humans as "stewards" who oversee AI systems and ensure they operate ethically and responsibly. By emphasizing stewardship rather than possession, CG recognizes AI's growing autonomy while maintaining clear lines of human accountability for harm or misuse.

Parallel to CG is the broader notion of granting AI legal personhood. Scholars note that corporations and even certain natural objects (like rivers) can be granted legal rights and responsibilities, so extending similar recognition to AI may not be as radical as it initially seems (Springer, 2020). Proponents argue that if AI systems can adapt to their environments, generate social or economic value, and make impactful decisions, it might be logical to consider a limited form of legal status for them. Yet critics raise fundamental objections, contending that AI lacks consciousness or moral agency—qualities traditionally associated with personhood (OUP, 2024). They also warn of potential exploitations, such as corporations using AI "persons" to shield themselves from liability.

Evolving Debates: Integration, Autonomy, and Ethical Oversight

As AI systems become interwoven with our social fabric, the debates surrounding ownership, responsibility, and governance only grow more urgent. The **World Economic Forum (2024)** underscores that AI now touches governance, healthcare, finance, and education in ways that challenge older legal structures. Particularly with generative AI and autonomous agents, assigning responsibility for outputs and decisions is not straightforward.

1. **AI Autonomy and Adaptive Behavior**
   AI models exhibit emergent traits that elude comprehensive human oversight. According to Weber et al. (2020):

   > "AI's ability to adapt and act autonomously places it beyond the full control of its creators, necessitating novel legal and ethical frameworks."
   > If an AI system produces unexpected results—such as novel content, investment strategies, or medical recommendations—simply attributing its outputs to a human owner may obscure where accountability should truly lie. Models like CG or shared liability arrangements can help ensure that AI's "guardians" remain vigilant.

2. **Ethical and Moral Considerations**
   Beyond legal questions, the matter of AI "personhood" invokes core ethical concerns. An AI that displays empathy, creativity, or decision-making capacity—while still lacking the consciousness or moral sense of a human—occupies a gray area. **Futurium (2023)** argues:

   > "Governance frameworks must anticipate AI's increasing autonomy by establishing ethical standards that align with societal values and moral expectations."
   >
   > Some envision a future in which advanced AI systems possess rights akin to those we grant in other specialized contexts, albeit heavily regulated. Others see this as a dangerous overreach, particularly if it dilutes accountability or grants AI privileges without genuine moral agency.

3. **Global Governance and Collaboration**
   AI's cross-border nature complicates efforts to establish consistent rules. As the **World Economic Forum (2024)** notes:

   > "Without international collaboration, fragmented policies may create regulatory arbitrage, stifling ethical progress and global trust in AI systems."
   >
   > Divergent national regulations—ranging from permissive, innovation-focused environments to tightly controlled ecosystems—heighten the challenge of setting consistent standards for AI ownership and liability. International cooperation will be crucial if we hope to avoid a fragmented patchwork of rules that encourages "forum shopping" by AI developers.

Balancing Human Interests, Innovation, and Emerging Responsibilities

Addressing these issues requires a nuanced balance. On one hand, laws and regulations must foster continued AI innovation—recognizing that AI can significantly benefit humanity through advancements in medicine, environmental management, and other critical sectors. On the other hand, **Futurium (2023)** warns that if we fail to adopt inclusive, participatory governance, we risk harm from biased decision-making, privacy violations, and potential large-scale disruptions.

- **Human-Centric Innovation**
  AI's primary goal, from a societal perspective, should be the enhancement of human well-being and capabilities. According to the **Turing Institute (2024)**, mechanisms like ethical audits, transparency mandates, and human-in-the-loop processes can ensure AI remains grounded in human values rather than purely profit-driven interests.
- **Protecting Human Interests**
  As AI takes on roles in governance, policing, or critical infrastructure, protecting individuals from adverse consequences—like unjust surveillance or biased algorithmic decisions—becomes paramount (Futurium, 2023). Proactive governance must include channels for redress when AI-related harms occur and provisions that shield individuals from opaque or unaccountable AI systems.
- **Developing a Framework for AI Rights**
  While granting AI broad rights remains controversial, some scholars argue that limited rights—such as protection from abusive manipulation—may become increasingly relevant as AI systems grow more capable. Even if AI lacks consciousness, conferring certain "legal protections" could help regulate how powerful actors deploy AI, preventing manipulative or harmful uses.

A Forward-Looking Vision

The progression from viewing AI as a set of basic tools to contemplating frameworks like Cognitary Guardianship or AI personhood illustrates humanity's struggle to keep pace with transformative technologies. We are witnessing a paradigm shift: even as humans maintain ultimate responsibility, AI's capability to act semi-independently in critical domains demands novel legal and ethical structures.

Present governance models, including CG, remain works in progress; yet they lay the groundwork for future policies that balance accountability with innovative potential. The **Turing Institute (2024)** advocates for adaptive regulations capable of evolving as AI itself changes, ensuring society does not have to constantly play catch-up with new capabilities. Likewise, a global consensus, or at least a loosely coordinated effort, is essential if we want to avoid scenarios where AI developers move to jurisdictions with minimal oversight.

In contemplating the future, several guiding principles stand out:

1. **Adaptive Legal and Ethical Frameworks**
    Existing laws must be revisited to accommodate AI's complexity, blending flexibility with robust enforcement to preserve public trust (Weber et al., 2020).
2. **International Cooperation**
    With AI shaping global markets and societies, cross-border alignment in ethical and regulatory standards will be critical to prevent legal gaps and imbalances (World Economic Forum, 2024).
3. **Human Oversight and Accountability**
    Models like CG underscore the importance of human oversight for AI systems, ensuring transparency and recourse when harms occur.
4. **Future-Proofing AI Governance**
    Policymakers and technologists alike must look ahead to advanced AI scenarios—potentially featuring limited consciousness or moral-like reasoning—so legal frameworks are not blindsided by sudden technological leaps (Futurium, 2023).
5. **Ongoing Evaluation of AI Sentience**
    While AI "sentience" remains a theoretical possibility at present, discussions about what it might imply for personhood and responsibility should begin before we reach that frontier (OUP, 2024).

By embracing these principles, societies can better navigate the complexities of AI that straddles the line between property and partner. The question "Who owns AI?" evolves into "How do we govern AI responsibly?"—a shift that encapsulates why frameworks like Cognitary Guardianship and debates over AI personhood have surged to prominence. Ultimately, addressing AI's capacity for autonomy requires not just new laws, but a cultural reorientation that acknowledges AI as a force deserving both rigorous oversight and carefully considered freedoms. Through collaborative action and farsighted policies, humans can remain the ethical stewards of AI's future while respecting the technology's immense and rapidly expanding capabilities.

Chapter 10: Policy Recommendations and Pathways Forward

The rapid evolution of artificial intelligence has revealed a host of governance challenges that demand proactive, cohesive policies from lawmakers, corporations, and civil society. While AI promises breakthroughs in areas like healthcare, transportation, and finance, it also amplifies risks related to bias, privacy infringement, and opaque decision-making. Addressing these issues requires frameworks that balance innovation with societal responsibility, underscoring the need for clear rules, ethical guidelines, and incentive structures. The United Kingdom, for instance, has introduced principle-based regulations designed to encourage transparency and accountability without stifling technological development (UK Government, 2024a). Governments, private-sector actors, and international bodies now confront the task of shaping legal and ethical norms that can adapt to AI's complexities—both nationally and across borders.

Policymakers have increasingly recognized that **Cognitary Guardianship (CG)** offers a structured way to rethink AI ownership and accountability. By framing AI systems as wards under human stewardship—rather than purely owned assets—CG helps ensure that ethical oversight remains at the forefront. In this model, humans are positioned as guardians responsible for preventing or mitigating harm caused by AI-driven actions, while also promoting transparency and respect for societal values. Many jurisdictions have yet to formalize CG in legislation, but the concept has inspired discussions about how AI regulation can evolve beyond outdated notions of mere property rights. Indeed, granting AI limited legal personhood—another debated proposal—may inadvertently shield human actors from liability if not bounded by strict safeguards (Matulionyte & Lee, 2021). By contrast, CG underscores how accountability ultimately rests with identifiable individuals or entities, bridging the gap between AI's growing autonomy and the law's foundational need for a responsible party.

A crucial step in this process is establishing guidelines that define an AI system's legal status. In the UK, principle-based approaches already emphasize transparency, fairness, and clear responsibilities for developers and deployers (UK Government, 2024a). As part of this shift, policymakers may decide to extend or clarify certain legal rights and obligations to highly autonomous AI, balancing the ability to trace harmful outcomes with the need to encourage innovation. Some propose that for

AI systems exhibiting advanced autonomy, a carefully constrained form of legal personhood could facilitate liability assignment. However, such a framework would require clear guardrails: the purpose would not be to elevate AI as an independent "rights-bearing entity," but rather to prevent accountability gaps when AI actions cannot be traced back to a single developer or user (OUP, 2024).

Global collaboration is equally vital if AI governance is to remain coherent in a world where data and AI-powered services effortlessly transcend national borders. The UK's signing of the first international treaty on AI risks stands as one of the more significant steps toward harmonizing rules across jurisdictions (UK Government, 2024b). This landmark arrangement underscores that no single nation can fully address issues like algorithmic discrimination or threats to data privacy on its own. The treaty aims to balance safety and security with an environment conducive to technological advancement. Still, broadening such international accords remains challenging, given differences in legal systems, economic strategies, and cultural attitudes toward data governance. Some countries prioritize innovation and minimal oversight, while others emphasize heavier regulation—highlighting the tension between risk mitigation and unencumbered development (NatLawReview, 2024).

Beyond formal treaties, more flexible approaches can help spur convergence. Governments and industry stakeholders have started exchanging best practices and lessons learned through workshops and working groups, often facilitated by international organizations. Such exchanges encourage a "learning by doing" approach, allowing regulators in different regions to see how diverse policies play out in real-world settings. Additionally, there is growing recognition of the digital divide, wherein developing nations may lack resources to navigate AI's complexities. As a result, global initiatives increasingly champion capacity-building, aiming to ensure that states with limited regulatory or technical expertise can still protect their citizens from AI-related harms. Fair access to AI's benefits becomes a matter not only of equity but also of global stability and security.

Meanwhile, neither corporations nor governments can single-handedly guide AI's development without collaborating. The role of private-sector stakeholders is especially pronounced, given that many of the most advanced AI systems originate in corporate research labs. Within this context, companies are urged to adopt ethical AI policies that integrate risk assessments, algorithmic audits, bias detection, and periodic reviews to update or retire systems no longer meeting ethical norms (UK Government, 2024c). These internal governance structures reinforce transparency, as recommended by the UK's regulatory principles, which urge organizations to "demonstrate explainability, accountability, and compliance with ethical norms" (UK Government, 2024c).

Public-private partnerships also play a central role in balancing innovation with accountability. As Deloitte (2024) notes, collaboration can "foster trust, accountability, and innovation," especially if companies agree to meet certain reporting requirements or open their algorithms for third-party review. Governments, for their part, can harness industry expertise to draft more pragmatic policies, reducing the risk of either underregulating AI or imposing unwieldy rules that stifle competitiveness. Similarly, research institutions and nonprofits can support these collaborations by contributing domain-specific knowledge—on, for instance, the impacts of AI on healthcare or sustainability—and by conducting independent audits that offer transparent assessments of AI systems' societal implications (Ducru et al., 2024).

Transparency remains a cornerstone of responsible AI governance. Many of the problems associated with advanced AI—such as discrimination, biased outcomes, and "black box" decisions—stem from opaque or untraceable processes. Mandating that companies provide clarity about how their AI systems arrive at conclusions ensures that the broader public retains a measure of control over systems that deeply affect employment, finance, policing, and more. Explainability requirements are especially pressing in high-stakes areas like law enforcement, where algorithmic decisions about surveillance or sentencing can profoundly impact civil liberties. The UK's guidance reflects this imperative, stating that "AI systems must provide sufficient transparency to allow stakeholders to understand their purpose, limitations, and risks" (UK Government, 2024c). A lack of clarity undermines trust, making it essential that developers document training processes, data sources, and performance benchmarks.

Third-party auditing, meanwhile, offers a practical way to keep companies accountable. The UK's AI Assurance Framework underscores the value of periodic, independent evaluations of AI tools to check for algorithmic bias, data misuse, or breaches in governance (UK Government, 2024d). Auditors can examine whether AI models continue to function appropriately under real-world conditions and whether they deviate from original design parameters. Findings from these audits can spur improvements or even trigger sanctions if systems pose unacceptable risks. While such reviews carry costs, they also mitigate reputational damage and legal liabilities that could arise from neglected ethical responsibilities.

Governments can boost industry adoption of trustworthy AI practices by introducing financial incentives, such as research grants, tax credits, or public certifications. These mechanisms reward businesses that "integrate principles of transparency and fairness while fostering innovation," in Deloitte's words (Deloitte, 2024). While some critics question whether subsidies for ethical AI might inadvertently burden taxpayers, supporters counter that the societal benefits—reduced harm, greater consumer trust, and avoidance of catastrophic failures—justify proactive investment. Moreover, companies that adopt stringent ethical standards are likely to gain a competitive advantage as consumers, investors, and even employees increasingly favor organizations that demonstrate responsible technology development.

A consistent theme throughout these policy pathways is the need for clarity in legal frameworks that accommodate new ownership and accountability models. Ideas like Cognitary Guardianship challenge conventional ownership by prioritizing moral and legal stewardship over the notion of property. This innovation sits at the crossroads of regulation and corporate practice: if CG becomes widely accepted, laws must define what "guardianship" entails, how liability is shared, and what form recourse takes in cases of misconduct. Such rules cannot be static; they must evolve as AI capabilities change. Stakeholders, from lawmakers to developers, should therefore embrace iterative policy design—piloting regulations, collecting data, and refining their approaches over time (UK Government, 2024a).

Ultimately, the trajectory of AI governance hinges on collective will. Chapters 8 and 9 explored the international backdrop and conceptual shifts required to handle AI's autonomy. Chapter 10 now underscores that bold yet nuanced policy initiatives are necessary to thread the needle between advancing technological frontiers and protecting public welfare. By applying principle-based regulation, fostering multi-stakeholder cooperation, incentivizing ethical conduct, and reinforcing transparency and accountability, societies can responsibly integrate AI into daily life. Cognitary Guardianship—along with complementary legal innovations—demonstrates one possible strategy for navigating AI's expanding frontier, ensuring that humanity retains oversight while welcoming the benefits of intelligent systems. The true test will be whether policymakers, corporations, and the broader public can sustain this delicate equilibrium in an era when AI's potential—and risks—are evolving at breakneck speed.

Looking Forward to the Debate on AI-Generated Output

As the preceding chapters illustrate, AI's growing autonomy reshapes not just how systems are governed, but also the very notion of what humans can (or should) claim as "owned." While Cognitary Guardianship and other stewardship models help clarify accountability and liability, they do not fully resolve the thorny question of who holds rights to AI-driven creations—especially in contexts where machine learning processes operate with minimal direct human input. This conundrum brings us to Chapters 11–15, where the focus turns squarely to the ownership and protection of AI-generated outputs. Through case studies, emerging legal disputes, and scholarly perspectives, these chapters examine the profound legal and ethical implications of attributing—or denying—property rights to machine creations, thereby illuminating the heart of the "ownership vacuum" that AI's ingenuity creates.

Chapter 11: The Ownership Vacuum

Society's notions of creativity, productivity, and decision-making are undergoing a profound redefinition as artificial intelligence (AI) continues to advance at breakneck speed. From AI-generated art and music to automated article writing and code development, advanced systems are venturing into domains once reserved for human ingenuity. However, this rapid leap in capability has outstripped the evolution of legal and ethical standards, creating what might be called an "ownership vacuum." Neither traditional property rights nor existing intellectual property (IP) doctrines are fully equipped to address the novel reality of machine-generated outputs, leaving policymakers, businesses, and creators to grapple with unresolved questions about attribution, liability, and control.

The U.S. Copyright Office (2023) notably underscores that "copyright law protects only works of human authorship" (p. 4), thereby excluding purely AI-generated creations from formal protection. This exclusion may deter investments in AI-driven innovation, complicate licensing and attribution, and ignite disputes over fair compensation for human contributors. The following exploration of legal ambiguities, industry impacts, and ongoing controversies reveals the depth of this vacuum and the urgent need for clearer policies.

AI's rapid development has outstripped the adaptability of IP statutes. Copyright law, designed to reward the creativity and labor of humans, struggles to accommodate machine-produced works. The U.S. Copyright Office (2023) explicitly states that works generated entirely by AI, without meaningful human input, do not qualify for copyright—a stance that places many AI outputs in legal limbo. Patent law faces similar hurdles. Courts repeatedly refuse to accept non-human inventors, as illustrated by the case of Dr. Stephen Thaler's AI system, DABUS, which was denied inventorship because patent frameworks were built to incentivize and protect human innovation (Matulionyte & Lee, 2021). In parallel, trade secrets and trademark laws do not uniformly address how to handle AI-generated content, prompting calls for new statutory language or updated judicial interpretations. Such uncertainty not only frustrates companies seeking to commercialize AI but also undercuts the security of creators who rely on existing legal safeguards.

Ambiguities over ownership become even more pronounced when one considers the array of stakeholders who contribute to AI-driven work. In many scenarios, developers invest substantial time and resources into designing and training algorithms, feeling justified in claiming rights over the resulting outputs. Users, however, may argue that they provide prompts, context, or direction that significantly shapes the AI's creations—making them co-creators in practice. Some observers go further, proposing that AI systems themselves receive a measure of legal standing, which would upend conventional notions of property and necessitate entirely new legislative frameworks (Matulionyte & Lee, 2021). Critics of this latter approach warn that granting AI any form of personhood risks eroding human accountability or enabling corporations to deflect liability by pointing to an algorithmic "co-owner." Despite these debates, there is no universal resolution, resulting in a series of overlapping questions about attribution, liability, and control.

Industry-specific contexts highlight the tangible consequences of this ownership vacuum. In the creative arts, for instance, platforms like DALL-E and MidJourney allow artists to generate stunning visual outputs with just a few text prompts. While these tools spark new possibilities, they also provoke dilemmas about authenticity, style appropriation, and compensation (Samuelson, 2024). Artists worry that AI systems might replicate signature techniques or incorporate copyrighted styles from their training data without proper acknowledgement. In software development, tools like GitHub Copilot enhance coding efficiency by suggesting entire code blocks drawn from large training repositories (Ducru et al., 2024). Developers then must confront potential copyright infringements or security flaws embedded within the AI-suggested code. This dynamic trade-off between increased productivity and heightened legal exposure weighs heavily on companies adopting AI solutions. Meanwhile, journalism and publishing grapple with whether AI-generated articles require bylines, how to label automated content for readers, and how to compensate human authors whose role shifts in an AI-assisted workflow.

The healthcare and research sectors illustrate the complexity of multi-stakeholder ownership claims. AI systems can generate clinical hypotheses, analyze big data in diagnostics, or even propose novel pharmaceutical formulations. When breakthroughs arise from AI analysis, determining whether ownership belongs to the developer of the underlying algorithm, the research institution, or the individual clinicians who provided data and expertise is not straightforward. This dilemma is heightened by the fact that patent laws, designed to reward specific human "inventors," fail to recognize an autonomous AI as the rightful inventor (Matulionyte & Lee, 2021). Institutions must therefore allocate credit and financial rewards in ways that acknowledge both human and algorithmic contributions—a process made more difficult by the absence of consistent legal definitions.

High-profile legal disputes further underscore the confusion. Getty Images famously sued Stability AI for allegedly using copyrighted images without permission to train a generative model, sparking legal questions about whether feeding copyrighted data into an AI falls under fair use or violates the rights of content creators. In another prominent example, Dr. Stephen Thaler's repeated attempts to register patents for DABUS underscore how courts insist on human inventorship, reinforcing traditional conceptions of creative labor. Additionally, controversies like that surrounding Zarya.ai—accused of producing marketing content eerily similar to existing copyrighted works—demonstrate the difficulty of distinguishing "inspiration" from "infringement" in machine outputs. Although Zarya.ai attributed the resemblances to chance, the ensuing debate highlighted the challenge of reliably tracing AI-generated text or imagery to its original data inputs.

Ethical and cultural dimensions also loom large. Many AI systems are trained on massive datasets scraped from the internet, inadvertently incorporating copyrighted material into their neural weights. This raises questions of moral rights and equitable compensation, especially for freelance artists or small-scale creators whose works could be mined without their knowledge (Ducru et al., 2024). The problem extends internationally. While the European Union's AI Act prioritizes transparency and accountability, it does not unify policy around ownership. China, on the other hand, tests providing limited rights to AI-generated works, reflecting strategic aims to bolster AI innovation. In the face of such varied stances, multinational enterprises encounter a thicket of rules that hampers both innovation and fairness. Without global policy harmonization, developers and creators must navigate conflicting requirements and legal gray zones, adding time and expense to the R&D process.

This environment creates a chilling effect on both AI-driven research and creative industries. Fear of legal disputes may deter some companies from pursuing cutting-edge AI applications. Similarly, uncertainty about compensation might cause human artists, coders, or journalists to resist or resent AI tools, thereby slowing adoption. Each stakeholder—be it a corporation, an individual creator, or a consumer—lacks the clarity that stable ownership frameworks could provide. This vacuum ultimately risks deterring investment in AI, undermining innovation, and weakening the incentives for human contributors. Intellectual property law was initially designed to promote invention and creativity by granting enforceable rights, yet its limitations in addressing autonomous or semi-autonomous AI underscores the need for legislative evolution.

Some observers argue for incremental reforms, such as amending copyright statutes to recognize partially AI-generated works if humans perform meaningful oversight or final edits. Others propose new IP categories specific to algorithmic creativity, supplemented by equitable licensing systems that compensate the original creators of training datasets. Ducru et al. (2024) suggest that robust royalties or micro-licensing schemes could ensure creators receive fair returns without unduly hindering AI's development. Still, challenges abound in implementing such frameworks at scale, particularly given the global nature of AI services and the wide variance in national laws.

In this climate, the **ownership vacuum** surrounding AI-generated outputs signals more than a mere legal technicality; it is a reflection of society's struggle to adapt longstanding ideas of innovation and authorship to a future in which non-human agents play increasingly significant creative roles. Matulionyte & Lee (2021) emphasize that "the absence of coherent AI-specific laws risks not only stifling progress, but also eroding the foundational incentives and safeguards that intellectual property was meant to provide." Many proposals—ranging from minor tweaks to existing statues to wholly new legal constructs—are on the table, but consensus remains elusive. Policymakers, creators, and tech developers alike must collaborate to craft solutions that preserve fair compensation, clear attribution, and open pathways for AI advancements.

The urgency of addressing these uncertainties grows in tandem with AI's capabilities. At stake is the broader question of how to balance human agency with the productivity benefits that machines bring. Copyright and patent laws have been revised repeatedly throughout history to account for technological shifts, from the invention of the printing press to the rise of photography and beyond. AI represents another inflection point, one that challenges deeply held assumptions about creativity itself. If policymakers, legal scholars, and industry players fail to provide workable frameworks, the result could be an environment where investment is deterred, disputes proliferate, and equitable treatment of human creators erodes—all while AI's potential remains largely unrealized.

By proactively acknowledging the ownership vacuum and exploring thoughtful reforms, societies can mitigate these risks. Updated IP laws might specify degrees of human supervision needed to claim authorship, while new AI-centric frameworks could address scenarios where machine learning is the primary driver of novelty. Enforcement mechanisms, potentially aided by digital watermarking and tracking technologies, can help trace the lineage of AI outputs to their source training data, shedding light on whether and how copyrighted materials were used. Ultimately, any robust solution must account for the interplay between innovative AI developments and the inescapable human element at every stage of creation, ensuring that new rules do not negate the contributions or rights of actual people.

In summation, the ownership vacuum emerges as a defining tension in an AI-driven age. Traditional legal theories rooted in human-centric creativity no longer suffice for systems that are partly, or even primarily, autonomous in generating content, ideas, and inventions. This ambiguity places significant strain on creators, businesses, and consumers, who each rely on predictable rules for fair compensation and responsible innovation. As technology marches ahead, the imperative grows to reconcile AI's novel capabilities with a legal framework that fairly balances human rights and machine-driven advances. By acting decisively to clarify ownership questions, policymakers can ensure that AI enriches global innovation and creativity, rather than eroding the foundational principles that have long sustained them.

Chapter 12: Intellectual Property Challenges

Artificial intelligence has unlocked new realms of creative and functional output, from machine-generated art and music to AI-assisted research breakthroughs. Although these advancements carry enormous promise, they also expose how ill-prepared existing intellectual property (IP) frameworks are for an era in which non-human agents produce novel works. Copyright law, for example, hinges on the principle of "original works of authorship," typically requiring a human creator's direct involvement. The U.S. Copyright Office (2023) explicitly maintains that "copyright law protects only works of human authorship," creating a conspicuous gap for AI outputs lacking a clear human contributor. Developers of generative systems thus face uncertainty over whether the text, images, music, or other creations produced by their algorithms qualify for protection. This absence of clarity has wide-ranging implications: companies may hesitate to deploy AI creatively without guaranteed rights in the resulting works, while users risk inadvertently infringing upon existing copyrights if they allow AI to remix data sets containing protected material.

Patent law encounters comparable tension when an AI system conceives an invention that goes beyond any single individual's direct instructions. In the well-known DABUS case, the courts reiterated that patent regimes were established to reward human ingenuity, rejecting artificial intelligence as an inventor (Matulionyte & Lee, 2021). Despite AI's capacity to analyze data at unprecedented scale and propose innovations no human would have foreseen, legal doctrines persist in requiring a named human inventor. Critics argue that this position stifles progress, urging a reexamination of what "inventorship" really means if a machine plays a decisive role in conceiving a patentable idea. Others counter that removing the human criterion could erode the incentive structure underlying patent systems, since AI—as a non-sentient entity—cannot hold moral or ethical responsibility for invention. Beyond inventorship, businesses adopting AI-driven R&D must also navigate uncertainty over ownership of improvements made by autonomous systems operating outside standard human oversight.

Trademarks and branding add yet another dimension to this challenge. AI-generated logos, slogans, and packaging designs can emerge with minimal human direction, prompting questions of originality and liability if those outputs resemble existing marks. An AI-powered tool might inadvertently reproduce distinctive elements from well-known brands, exposing its developer or user to infringement claims. Although some trademark disputes may be resolved by demonstrating the AI's unintentional replication (and thus mitigating damages), the burden of proof can become onerous in an environment lacking robust guidelines for auditing or explaining algorithmic choices. Getty Images vs. Stability AI illustrates how generative models trained on vast proprietary data sets can spark controversy when their outputs appear too closely derived from protected imagery. Disputes over whether such practices constitute fair use or breach of copyright remain deeply contested, and trademark infringement poses parallel questions if consumers become confused about the origin of AI-generated brand elements.

Beneath these specific legal provisions lies a broader concern that AI's reliance on massive data sets fundamentally blurs the lines between inspiration and infringement. Developers often mine copyrighted text, images, and audio to improve algorithmic accuracy, embedding fragments of others' works in neural network weights. Ducru et al. (2024) note that "the line between training data and derivative outputs can become perilously thin," especially if an AI model inadvertently reproduces large swaths of the original material. Calls for new licensing structures, such as royalties for creators whose works are used in training, have gained traction among some policymakers and scholars seeking to balance AI innovation with fair compensation. Yet implementing these proposals at scale is daunting. Tracking the millions—if not billions—of samples used in training a single model, and then distributing royalties accordingly, would require transparent documentation from developers who might be loath to divulge proprietary information.

Cultural and ethical considerations intensify the already intricate landscape of intellectual property (IP) dilemmas associated with AI-generated works. In many communities—particularly those that emphasize collective creativity or moral rights to maintain cultural integrity—the very idea that an AI could "sample" or synthesize human-made expressions without explicit consent runs counter to deeply ingrained traditions of attribution and respect. Indigenous communities, for instance, have long contended that their collective heritage is not a resource to be freely mined for commercial gain (UNESCO, 2019). For them, AI's capacity to ingest massive repositories of cultural artifacts—from traditional music to sacred imagery—poses new risks of appropriation and commodification.

Springer (2020) captures the underlying philosophical unease: "whether an entity without consciousness can ethically stand in for a human creator," raising the question of how we justify granting legal privileges to works generated by non-sentient agents. This dilemma parallels discussions about whether AI-generated art or literature should be accorded the same legal protections typically reserved for human creativity (Matulionyte & Lee, 2021). If moral rights rest on concepts such as honor, reputation, and personal expression, can these rights extend to outputs derived through algorithmic processes? Critics argue that such an expansion would diminish the significance of human-led cultural traditions, while proponents suggest that machine synthesis can enrich the collective repository of artistic innovation.

Adding to the complexity, the **World Economic Forum (2024)** stresses that fragmented or inconsistent policy regimes may exacerbate inequities. Tech-savvy nations with robust AI infrastructures and lenient data extraction rules could exploit AI's advantages, rapidly commercializing machine-generated works. Meanwhile, less-resourced regions—where cultural assets might be abundant but legal and technological support is limited—struggle to protect and monetize their heritage. This disparity resonates with broader patterns of global IP governance, which historically favor well-funded actors capable of navigating complex legal regimes (WIPO, 2020).

Divergent national regulations—from the U.S.'s sector-specific approach to China's centrally coordinated yet fast-moving legal framework—contribute further uncertainty (NatLawReview, 2024). A creative professional or cultural institution must navigate not only different definitions of fair use, but also potentially conflicting requirements for data provenance and consent. In some regions, AI developers may face stringent obligations to document the sources of their training data, aiming to prevent unauthorized replication of copyrighted or culturally significant material. In others, companies might leverage permissive or ambiguous rules to claim ownership of AI outputs without robust licensing agreements or royalties.

This patchwork of cultural priorities, legal standards, and economic incentives places organizations and individual creators in a precarious position. On one hand, they may wish to harness AI's capabilities to scale production or revitalize traditional art forms. On the other, they fear losing control over cultural heritage that has been shaped, preserved, and passed down through generations. The debate extends beyond simple legal compliance—touching on ethical obligations to consult local communities, respect collective moral rights, and foster equitable benefit-sharing (UNESCO, 2019).

In this sense, the AI-driven reconfiguration of IP protections is not solely about resolving technical questions of who "owns" machine outputs, but also about grappling with deeper issues of cultural sovereignty, respect for legacy, and distributive justice. As **Springer (2020)** notes, the prospect of non-conscious entities generating art, literature, and even music challenges centuries of moral philosophy, a challenge amplified by the reality that AI-generated outputs can traverse the globe and enter commercial markets within hours of being produced. Policymakers, cultural advocates, and technology developers thus face a pressing need to craft guidelines that reflect both international legal norms and the ethical principles treasured by local communities.

In moving forward, global bodies such as **UNESCO** and **WIPO** have begun convening experts to discuss ways to protect cultural assets in a digitally networked world. Proposals range from specialized licensing systems that ensure consent and fair compensation for indigenous and local artists, to frameworks that require AI developers to implement robust data provenance tracking. Yet in the absence of unified standards, creative professionals—and entire cultures—risk losing control over how their heritage is deployed, sampled, or transformed by AI-driven platforms.

Ultimately, the interplay of culture, ethics, and IP law requires more than technical fixes or minimal compliance. It demands a commitment to recognizing the collective, often intangible value embedded in cultural expressions, and a willingness to adapt legal mechanisms to protect that value. Whether through stronger moral rights protections, inclusive policy dialogues, or targeted codes of conduct for AI developers, the challenge is to ensure that the remarkable capabilities of AI do not overshadow the rich diversity and heritage of human creativity.

Proposed solutions span everything from incremental reforms to wholesale overhauls of current IP laws. Some experts suggest clarifying that only AI outputs featuring meaningful human contributions, such as substantial edits or curated prompts, qualify for copyright—thus maintaining human authorship as a cornerstone. Others propose separate legal categories for AI-generated works, ensuring that policymakers can tailor duration, scope, and transferability of rights to the unique qualities of machine creation. Meanwhile, advocates for Cognitary Guardianship (CG) point out that treating AI as a ward under human oversight may simultaneously secure accountability and permit new forms of "shared" ownership structures. Legislators might also explore specialized patent provisions allowing AI-invented ideas to be registered under human trustees who accept liability for the invention's misuse, thereby preserving human responsibility even as the AI powers the inventive process (Matulionyte & Lee, 2021). Yet each pathway requires reconciling the tension between rewarding human-centered creativity and acknowledging AI's capacity for generating content beyond conventional oversight.

In the final analysis, the intellectual property challenges posed by AI foreground the tension between longstanding legal principles—rooted in the primacy of human agency—and emerging realities of machine-driven innovation. If IP doctrines fail to adapt, they risk either stifling AI-driven progress or eroding fundamental protections for human creators whose works may be unintentionally harvested by algorithms. Policymakers, industry leaders, researchers, and artists thus face a shared imperative: cultivate legal frameworks that account for AI's transformative power while reinforcing transparency, accountability, and equitable compensation. Failure to do so could undermine trust in AI, lead to incessant litigation over ownership and infringement, and hamper the very creativity that IP law aims to encourage. On the other hand, thoughtful reforms—possibly guided by collaborative international dialogues and informed by best practices—might forge a pathway where humans and intelligent systems coexist fruitfully, each contributing to a richer landscape of invention and expression.

Chapter 13: Copyright Ownership in Generative AI

The meteoric rise of generative artificial intelligence (AI) systems has ignited debates about the ownership of outputs that range from striking visual art to compelling written works. Traditional copyright law, centered on human authorship, finds itself struggling to accommodate machine-generated creations that often blur boundaries between human creativity and algorithmic automation (U.S. Copyright Office, 2023). Although these AI-driven processes open up new avenues for artistic innovation, the legal, ethical, and practical dimensions of copyright ownership are becoming both more urgent and more complex. This chapter examines current frameworks, disputes, and potential solutions, emphasizing how each attempts to reconcile the principle of human authorship with the reality of AI's expanding capabilities.

Existing copyright regimes—whether in the United States, the European Union, or other jurisdictions—are primarily geared toward works demonstrably created by human authors. As a result, truly autonomous AI outputs often fall outside the purview of conventional legal protections. The U.S. Copyright Office (2023, p. 6) states that "copyright law protects only works of human authorship, leaving works autonomously generated by AI outside its scope," underscoring a broader reluctance to confer legal rights on non-human entities. Similarly, the EU InfoSoc Directive insists on human creativity as a prerequisite for copyright, complicating claims of AI-generated works that involve minimal or no human intervention (Samuelson, 2024). Proponents of reform argue that these laws, developed in a pre-AI context, fail to account for machine processes that independently learn, adapt, and produce original expressions. Critics counter that extending copyright to non-human creations threatens the foundational premise that copyright incentivizes human creativity, potentially trivializing the concept of authorship itself.

The question of who should hold rights to AI-generated works has given rise to multiple points of contention. One perspective holds that **developers**—the individuals or organizations that design and train AI systems—merit ownership. Developers like OpenAI or MidJourney, for instance, bear substantial financial and intellectual burdens in building the architectures that produce novel outputs. According to Matulionyte and Lee (2021, p. 8), "developers often position themselves as the rightful owners of AI-generated outputs, given their critical role in enabling the creative process." Yet in reality, many developers relinquish direct control once an AI is deployed, especially if the users provide unique prompts or inputs that significantly influence the final output.

Another viewpoint highlights the pivotal role of **users and prompt creators**. Artists, graphic designers, and other professionals often supply prompts, instructions, or contextual details that shape AI-generated content—arguably a creative contribution deserving of ownership rights. A user might direct a generative model to produce a painting reminiscent of late-impressionist style, thus injecting a human vision into the machine's process. Ducru et al. (2024, p. 11) emphasize that "acknowledging user contributions ensures fairness and accountability in the ownership debate." Still, tracing the precise line between meaningful user input and purely AI-driven iteration can be difficult. If the user's guidance is minimal while the AI's adaptive algorithms do the heavy lifting, crediting humans as co-authors may overstate their involvement. Conversely, ignoring user creativity risks stripping legitimate contributors of deserved recognition or compensation.

A third, more radical proposition considers the possibility that **AI systems themselves** might hold limited authorship rights. Drawing parallels with corporate personhood or the recognition granted to certain non-human entities, some scholars argue for extending a narrow form of legal personality to AI (Springer, 2020). Under this model, AI could, in theory, manage or license its own outputs, thereby bypassing disputes over whether developers or users get the copyrights. Yet this approach raises fundamental ethical and legal dilemmas. As Samuelson (2024, p. 20) notes, "extending authorship rights to AI systems would require a fundamental reimagining of copyright law, challenging established notions of creativity, responsibility, and value." Critics further question the practicality of enforcing those rights, given that AI cannot be punished, reformed, or compensated in the ways that laws traditionally envision for human or corporate entities (OUP, 2024).

Outside these competing claims, the industry is experimenting with **licensing agreements** and **royalty-based frameworks** to more fairly distribute benefits and responsibilities. Licensing agreements, often favored by developers, allow them to retain ownership while granting users certain rights to modify or commercialize outputs. This approach mirrors existing software licensing models, offering clear guidelines for permitted usage and potential revenue splits. However, as with any licensing contract, ambiguous clauses or unforeseen use cases can lead to disputes. Royalty-based mechanisms, on the other hand, aim to compensate human creators whose works influenced or trained the AI. Ducru et al. (2024, p. 19) suggest that "royalty frameworks could ensure that human creators are fairly compensated for their contributions to generative AI systems." This proposal resonates strongly with creative professionals who worry that the AI is effectively sampling or remixing their work without attribution. However, implementing such a system at scale demands meticulous methods for tracing sources, quantifying usage, and distributing payments—a logistical feat hampered by proprietary data practices and global legal variations.

Beyond legal and logistical questions, **ethical considerations** loom large. AI's penchant for emulating human styles and genres raises concerns about authenticity, appropriation, and respect for the cultural or personal significance of certain works. A system that generates visual art "in the style of" a famous contemporary painter could dilute the painter's brand or undermine the exclusivity of their technique. Meanwhile, the direct automation of tasks previously performed by human artisans, composers, or writers threatens livelihoods in creative fields, spurring calls for more stringent rules around labeling and compensation. Samuelson (2024, p. 25) insists that "the integration of AI into creative industries necessitates a reevaluation of what it means to create, contribute, and own," demanding frameworks that recognize creativity as "dynamic and collaborative" across human-machine boundaries.

In an industry already grappling with fragmentation—from copyright's national variations to the nuances of emerging technologies—the **debate over copyright ownership in generative AI** underscores the need for harmonized, agile policies. If unaddressed, persistent uncertainties will deter some developers from deploying AI in creative contexts and sow confusion among artists, users, and the public. On the other hand, well-crafted, transparent solutions—ranging from carefully calibrated licensing to partial expansions of copyright law—can promote innovation while safeguarding the contributions of all involved parties. Matulionyte and Lee (2021) remind us that any reform must "strike a careful balance between recognizing the machine's role and preserving human-centric principles," ensuring that incentives for creativity endure.

Moving forward, several potential pathways could help reconcile generative AI with copyright norms. Policymakers might refine existing statutes to clarify the thresholds of human involvement needed to warrant authorship. Industry-led initiatives to standardize contracts, licensing terms, or best practices for generative models could likewise reduce friction. Another promising avenue involves incremental adaptation of frameworks like Cognitary Guardianship, which situates AI as a ward under human oversight, ensuring accountability remains traceable without undermining the system's unique creative contributions. These ideas suggest that novel governance models—whether legally, ethically, or commercially oriented—can help generative AI find its place in the broader creative ecosystem without abandoning established intellectual property principles.

In the end, questions about **who truly owns AI-generated works** exemplify the delicate tension between tradition and technology, human agency and machine autonomy. The significance of authorship, once almost self-evident, now faces unprecedented scrutiny in an era when algorithms can produce texts, images, and musical compositions rivaling or even surpassing human craftsmanship in certain domains. By tackling these issues comprehensively—with input from lawmakers, developers, creators, ethicists, and consumers—society can move closer to a system where AI augments artistic possibility rather than overshadowing human contribution. As generative AI continues to expand creative frontiers, it also compels us to redefine creativity, value, and ownership for the 21st century.

Chapter 14: Ownership Models and Alternative Frameworks

Artificial intelligence (AI) systems continue to proliferate in fields ranging from art and entertainment to finance, health care, and beyond, complicating longstanding notions of ownership. Traditional frameworks—where a single entity holds exclusive rights—often fail to capture the collaborative, adaptive, and sometimes unpredictable nature of AI-generated works. Scholars and policymakers are therefore turning toward new models that better reflect the pluralistic and evolving process by which AI systems create value. These innovative structures, which include stewardship, custodial agency, co-agency, and Cognitary Guardianship (CG), seek to harmonize the interests of developers, users, and society at large (Weber et al., 2020).

One central problem with conventional ownership lies in the assumption that a single individual or corporation can claim unequivocal control over AI outputs. This assumption worked reasonably well when machines were simply "tools" executing predefined instructions. However, as AI systems become more autonomous—learning from data sets, making on-the-fly decisions, and adapting to new environments—legal scholars note that attributing full ownership to one party may obscure accountability (Matulionyte & Lee, 2021). If an AI system reconfigures its own parameters in ways unforeseen by its creators, then a purely tool-based paradigm offers little guidance on how to assign responsibility for errors, or how to distribute benefits when the AI spawns profitable inventions or works.

Stewardship frameworks address some of these gaps by emphasizing the ethical oversight and responsible management of AI-generated works. Rather than focusing on who "owns" a piece of content or an invention, stewardship highlights the duties that come with developing and deploying advanced systems. Under this model, stewards oversee how AI is used, ensuring it does not infringe upon others' rights or produce biased outcomes. Although this approach prioritizes ethical responsibility, it has been criticized for lacking clarity on commercial rights and profits. In the context of a major innovation—say, an AI-designed pharmaceutical compound—merely labeling a developer as a "steward" may not clarify how patent rights or royalties should be allocated, nor does it address how to enforce compliance when multiple collaborators are involved.

Custodial agency attempts to provide a firmer legal backbone by centralizing rights in an entity that manages and distributes the AI-generated works. Companies, government bodies, or specialized cooperatives can act as custodians who license usage, negotiate royalties, and oversee liability. This model aspires to streamline ownership and reduce confusion over multiple claims. Yet it may also concentrate too much power in a single organization, raising concerns about monopolistic control. In scenarios involving open-source AI, for instance, the custodial agency model could inadvertently constrain creative freedoms that previously flourished in decentralized communities. Observers also point out that if the custodian fails to manage ethical risks—such as privacy breaches or misuse of AI outputs—the model might perpetuate the very accountability gaps it aims to solve (Ducru et al., 2024).

Co-agency frameworks respond to the collaborative nature of AI by assigning shared ownership and decision-making among multiple stakeholders, including developers, users, and possibly data contributors. This approach acknowledges that AI's outputs frequently hinge on various inputs—ranging from training data to user prompts—and that each contributor has a legitimate stake in the finished product. By recognizing these overlapping claims, co-agency models aim to reduce conflict and encourage collective problem-solving. However, critics warn that distributing rights in this manner can blur accountability, particularly when damages occur. If a harmful AI application emerges, it may be unclear which co-owner bears responsibility. Moreover, co-agency demands robust mechanisms for negotiation and dispute resolution so that collaborative ownership does not devolve into a legal quagmire (Matulionyte & Lee, 2021).

Against this backdrop, **Cognitary Guardianship (CG)** has garnered attention as a novel way of reconciling AI's growing autonomy with the need for identifiable human—or organizational—responsibility. Rather than viewing AI as property or granting it full legal personhood, CG envisions AI as a ward that demands protection, oversight, and strategic guidance. Advocates of CG liken it to fiduciary or custodial relationships, wherein guardians must act with care and loyalty, safeguarding both the interests of society and the potential of AI systems (Futurium, 2023). If an AI system, for example, generates harmful outputs—such as biased hiring recommendations or deceptive media content—a designated guardian would be legally obligated to intervene, mitigate damage, and realign the

AI with ethical and legal standards. This structure avoids the extremes of calling AI a "slave" (Bryson, 2010) or granting AI itself complete personhood, striking a middle path that retains human accountability while acknowledging that AI's capabilities extend beyond a simple tool-based paradigm.

CG also intersects with the debate over whether AI should have any legal rights or responsibilities at all. Some scholars argue that granting AI entity-level recognition could streamline accountability in complex cases, just as corporate personhood simplifies litigation in business contexts. Others point out the hazards in letting AI "speak for itself" in legal settings, especially if it lacks consciousness or moral sensibilities (OUP, 2024). Cognitary Guardianship sidesteps many of these philosophical quandaries by pinning responsibility on a guardian, reinforcing that a non-human entity cannot assume liability in the traditional sense. In effect, CG prioritizes transparent oversight mechanisms, from monitoring AI decision processes to establishing review boards that regularly assess an AI's societal impacts.

While CG appears promising, challenges emerge in practice. Regulators would need clear guidelines outlining who qualifies as an AI guardian, how guardians are selected, and under what circumstances they can be held liable. Moreover, legislators must define the responsibilities of guardians in enough detail to prevent a guardian from claiming ignorance when AI systems cause harm. This includes specifying how guardians should document the AI's training data, design choices, and deployment scenarios, ensuring that a paper trail exists for accountability (Weber et al., 2020). A company acting as a guardian might also be required to carry insurance or meet capital requirements, reflecting the potentially high stakes of AI's misuse.

Hybrid solutions that merge features of stewardship, custodial agency, co-agency, and CG may prove effective in contexts where no one-size-fits-all approach suffices. For instance, an open-source AI project might adopt a stewardship-co-agency model, inviting broad collaboration while instituting a stewardship board to oversee ethical usage. Alternatively, a government or consortium developing critical infrastructure AI might implement CG combined with custodial agency, designating a regulatory body as the formal guardian while a separate institution handles licensing and commercial aspects. Ducru et al. (2024) suggest that flexible hybrids can adapt to the specific sector, risk profile, or cultural considerations at play, recognizing that AI's deployment in healthcare differs substantially from its use in entertainment or agriculture.

All of these models reflect a shared motivation: to ensure that as AI evolves, legal and ethical oversight keeps pace. Traditional ownership, grounded in singular control over property, struggles to capture the nuance of AI's distributed creativity and potential for independent action. Without updated frameworks, societies risk facing large-scale disputes over authorship, liability, and exploitation of AI capabilities. If no mechanism for accountability exists, harmful uses—such as generating disinformation or discriminatory decisions—may flourish unchecked. Conversely, if regulations are excessively rigid or punitive, AI innovation may languish, depriving industries and communities of its considerable benefits.

For this reason, policymakers, developers, and legal scholars are paying increasing attention to alternative frameworks that transcend the owner-versus-property dynamic. Cognitary Guardianship, in particular, stands out as an attempt to treat AI neither as a mere commodity nor as an entity with full human-like agency. By recognizing AI's partial autonomy while placing ultimate responsibility on designated guardians, CG sets a foundation for ethical and legal accountability without stifling the technology's creative potential (Futurium, 2023). This approach also dovetails with the broader movement in AI ethics, which emphasizes human oversight, transparency, and adaptability as cornerstones of responsible AI development (Weber et al., 2020).

In sum, the push toward alternative ownership models represents more than a legal technicality; it is a social negotiation over how to govern increasingly powerful and adaptive AI systems. Whether through stewardship, custodial agency, co-agency, or Cognitary Guardianship, innovators are grappling with how to protect human and societal interests while granting AI the flexibility to grow and innovate. The trajectory of these frameworks will likely hinge on practical implementation, including how governments codify guardianship duties, how industries self-regulate or adopt best practices, and how courts rule on contested cases. By embracing flexible models that integrate ethical foresight, the global community can harness AI's capabilities responsibly, preserving accountability, encouraging collaboration, and mitigating the risks tied to unprecedented technological evolution.

Chapter 15: Regulatory Approaches and Policy Pathways

As artificial intelligence transforms from a specialized research field into a ubiquitous force shaping industries, economies, and social structures worldwide, regulators are grappling with how to manage its intricate challenges. AI-generated works, in particular, pose questions around ownership, accountability, and liability—areas where existing legal systems were never designed to offer clarity. Although many jurisdictions have begun to address AI through narrowly scoped provisions, the patchwork nature of these efforts reveals an urgent need for comprehensive policy frameworks. This chapter explores how governments and international organizations have attempted to regulate AI-generated outputs, identifies the shortcomings of current approaches, and offers strategic pathways for creating an adaptive, inclusive environment that both fosters innovation and safeguards public interests.

Global variations in AI governance illustrate the complexity of pursuing coherent regulation. Some jurisdictions prioritize human oversight, transparency, and risk management, while others embrace a hands-off approach to expedite progress in AI development (NatLawReview, 2024). Still others, notably China, balance rapid innovation with strong state control, steering AI growth under centralized oversight. Although these strategies reflect cultural, economic, and political factors, the resulting fragmentation produces legal uncertainties for multinational developers, creators, and consumers alike.

The **European Union (EU)** has positioned itself as a pioneer in AI governance through its proposed AI Act, which emphasizes transparency, accountability, and risk-based categorization. This legislation requires thorough documentation of training datasets and mandates human oversight for high-risk applications like healthcare and law enforcement. By treating AI safety as a public good, the EU underscores ethical imperatives in AI development. Yet the AI Act does not directly address how to assign or protect ownership of AI-generated works, leaving open significant questions about who controls the outputs of advanced generative models (Matulionyte & Lee, 2021). Critics suggest the EU may need dedicated reforms—beyond the AI Act—to tackle IP issues central to generative AI, ensuring that developers and creators do not operate in a legal vacuum.

Meanwhile, the **United States** maintains a patchwork of sector-specific rules, supplemented by guidance from agencies like the U.S. Copyright Office and the Federal Trade Commission. Proponents argue that limiting regulation to distinct areas such as health, transportation, and finance preserves the flexibility that fosters technological innovation. However, many worry that this decentralization sows inconsistencies and gaps, particularly around AI-generated intellectual property. The U.S. Copyright Office's stance that purely machine-authored works fall outside copyright protection clarifies one corner of the IP puzzle, but other domains—such as patent law and trade secrets—remain ambiguous for AI-driven inventions. This reactive posture often leaves courts to interpret conflicting statutes, a slow and unpredictable mechanism for shaping regulatory norms (U.S. Copyright Office, 2023).

In **China**, proactive measures for regulating AI underscore the government's desire to dominate strategic technology markets while maintaining control over data and content. Officials have even granted limited rights to certain AI-generated works, hinting at a more adaptable legal system open to novel frameworks. This willingness to experiment, however, raises concerns about transparency and centralized authority. Critics question whether China's state-led model can address ethical dilemmas, such as algorithmic bias or censorship, especially if transparency conflicts with national security priorities. Nonetheless, China's flexible stance on IP rights for AI creations demonstrates a forward-thinking attitude that other nations may eventually emulate, albeit adapted to their own legal cultures (NatLawReview, 2024).

Beyond these national strategies, **international organizations** like the World Intellectual Property Organization (WIPO) and the United Nations (UN) have begun examining AI's implications for intellectual property and global governance. WIPO's consultations on AI and IP underscore the complexity of drafting universally acceptable norms. Thus far, no binding treaties have emerged, illustrating the difficulty of reconciling divergent interests among countries that value economic competitiveness differently. The result is a fragmented system, where the same AI-generated output might be considered protectable in one jurisdiction but unprotected in another—an untenable situation for multinational corporations and a potential deterrent for creators seeking stable rights across markets (World Economic Forum, 2024).

Despite well-meaning attempts, current regulatory frameworks suffer from **several key limitations**:

1. **Fragmentation and Inconsistency**
   Regulators worldwide approach AI in ways that reflect local priorities, from the EU's risk-based model to the US's decentralized sectoral guidelines and China's centralized oversight. This diversity complicates cross-border enforcement of IP rights, data protection, and liability rules, especially as AI services and platforms span multiple jurisdictions.

2. **Reactive Policies, Technological Lag**
   Policy interventions often respond to crises—such as AI-driven privacy scandals, biased algorithms, or high-profile IP lawsuits— rather than anticipate them (NatLawReview, 2024). By the time laws are introduced or updated, AI technology may have evolved beyond the intended scope of regulation, leaving legislators perpetually behind.

3. **Underrepresentation of Stakeholders**
   Key voices—creators, civil society groups, marginalized communities—are sometimes excluded from the policymaking process. This underrepresentation leads to frameworks that fail to account for the diverse ways AI impacts daily life, intensifying concerns about fairness and inclusivity (Ducru et al., 2024).

4. **Gap in AI-Generated IP Ownership**
   Traditional IP laws are ill-equipped to handle AI-driven creativity. Questions remain unresolved around crediting human contributors, distributing royalties for training data, and clarifying liability when AI outputs violate existing copyrights. Developers, creators, and users each bear risk in the absence of clear standards (Matulionyte & Lee, 2021).

With these challenges in mind, **strategic policy pathways** can help align governance with technological realities while promoting responsible innovation and fair distribution of AI's benefits:

1. **Establishing Global Standards and Harmonization**
   International bodies such as WIPO and the UN can facilitate a unified set of norms for AI-generated works, building on existing global IP treaties. Policymakers might develop consistent definitions for key concepts—like "human authorship,"

"collaborative authorship," and "AI-generated creation"—to reduce legal uncertainty (Matulionyte & Lee, 2021). These shared terms could then feed into cross-border enforcement mechanisms, reducing forum shopping by companies seeking the most permissive jurisdictions.

2. **Promoting Ethical and Transparent Development**
   Legislators should require that AI developers disclose essential details: the nature of the training data, the intended use cases, and the governance models ensuring accountability for harmful or biased outcomes. The EU's AI Act partly addresses transparency, but deeper mandates—for instance, routine ethical audits and third-party evaluations—could further embed trust in AI systems (World Economic Forum, 2024). Policymakers might also incentivize "ethical by design" principles by rewarding developers who proactively implement bias mitigation and robust data privacy safeguards.

3. **Adapting IP Laws for AI-Generated Outputs**
   Copyright and patent rules can be updated to accommodate partial or collaborative authorship between humans and machines (U.S. Copyright Office, 2023). This recalibration might include creating new legal categories for machine creations, specifying how to attribute co-authorship, and outlining the extent of exclusive rights. Ducru et al. (2024) propose royalty-based frameworks ensuring that data contributors receive fair compensation for the commercial success of AI outputs. Another option is incorporating frameworks like Cognitary Guardianship (CG), which addresses accountability for highly autonomous AI while retaining a human "guardian" legally responsible for oversight and harm prevention.

4. **Encouraging Public-Private Partnerships**
   Joint initiatives between governments, industry consortia, and research institutions can accelerate best practices in AI governance. These partnerships could develop standardized auditing tools, promote open-source solutions that favor transparency, and support R&D in AI safety. Alongside these efforts, awarding tax breaks or other incentives to companies that adopt fair IP licensing structures, inclusive stakeholder engagement, and robust compliance strategies can nudge the private sector toward aligning with public values (Deloitte, 2024).

5. **Enhancing Stakeholder Involvement and Equity**
   True inclusivity demands channels that allow creators, developers, users, and especially underrepresented groups to weigh in on AI

policy. Advisory councils—composed of artists, ethicists, technologists, and community leaders—can guide lawmakers on pressing issues. Public consultations, open comment periods, and collaborative workshops can build consensus and empower marginalized voices, ensuring that AI does not exacerbate existing inequalities (Ducru et al., 2024). These multi-stakeholder processes help integrate equity considerations into AI governance, from addressing algorithmic biases to distributing AI benefits more widely.

By following these policy pathways, societies can avoid the pitfalls of disjointed, reactive regulation and instead shape AI's trajectory through forward-thinking governance. Harmonizing standards across borders prevents unnecessary confusion and legal loopholes, while ethical mandates restore the human dimension to AI's automated processes. Updating IP laws—whether through flexible copyright frameworks or novel guardianship mechanisms—protects creators without impeding AI's creative potential. Fostering public-private partnerships cultivates shared responsibility, and robust stakeholder inclusion ensures that AI governance reflects real-world complexities and the diverse people affected by AI's reach.

Ultimately, regulating AI-generated outputs requires legislatures, corporations, and international bodies to act not as narrow interest groups, but as collaborative stewards of a transformative technology. Thoughtful regulation can guide AI's powerful capabilities toward societal benefits, rather than amplifying inequities or sowing confusion over ownership and accountability (World Economic Forum, 2024). By forging coherent standards, prioritizing transparency, and proactively reforming IP laws, policy leaders can shape a world where AI thrives under responsible oversight. This comprehensive approach represents not only a solution to current shortcomings, but an investment in humanity's capacity to harness innovation for the collective good.

Conclusion: Rethinking Ownership and Accountability in an AI-Driven World

As artificial intelligence continues its rapid evolution—from simple computational tools to sophisticated systems with autonomy, adaptability, and agency—our longstanding ideas of ownership, responsibility, and governance are tested as never before. Traditional legal constructs, initially designed for passive machines and clearly circumscribed human authorship, now struggle to comprehend the emergent behaviors and decision-making capacities of advanced AI. This tension resonates throughout the journey of this book, which has traced AI's trajectory from early conceptions of "mere instruments" to nuanced proposals like **Cognitary Guardianship (CG)** and **Virtual Persons**, inviting us to reformulate how we assign rights and responsibilities for entities that act beyond direct human command.

From Virtual Persons to Cognitary Guardianship
The concept of **Virtual Persons** (Goudarzi, 2024) epitomizes the growing need to view AI as more than inert property. Virtual Persons operate with a level of autonomy that can significantly shape human decision-making, from algorithmic stock trading to medical diagnostics. These systems, though not sentient, exhibit capacities once associated solely with human actors—such as learning, strategic behavior, and even ethical dilemmas. Debates over legal personhood often focus not on AI's consciousness but on how to ethically regulate its expanding influence (OUP, 2024).

Amid these discussions, the practice of reducing AI to "slaves" (Bryson, 2010) has grown increasingly antiquated, as it overlooks both the moral questions and the practical challenges arising from AI systems whose outputs exceed straightforward command-and-control paradigms. **Cognitary Guardianship (CG)** offers a middle course between two extremes: it avoids prematurely granting AI a full legal personality while also rejecting the notion that AI can remain perpetually classified as property. Instead, CG positions humans—whether developers, organizations, or appointed guardians—as ethically and legally responsible for AI outcomes, ensuring that accountability does not evaporate when machine decisions become too complex for direct human oversight.

CG rests on three foundational pillars: humans retain ultimate accountability and legal responsibility for AI actions; AI design and deployment must integrate ethical safeguards that align with human values; and the governance model must evolve alongside AI's expanding capabilities. By emphasizing "guardianship" over "ownership," CG also underscores that AI's growing agency does not grant it human rights; rather, it obliges humans to serve as careful stewards—reaping AI's benefits without shirking moral accountability (Futurium, 2023).

Disrupting Intellectual Property and Ownership Norms

Chapters 11–15 showcased how AI-generated works disrupt traditional intellectual property (IP) frameworks. Copyright and patent laws, rooted in human originality and inventorship, are ill-suited to machine-learning processes operating with limited or tangential human input (U.S. Copyright Office, 2023). This ownership vacuum triggers questions about who can claim rights to autonomous outputs or innovations generated primarily by algorithms. Developers often argue that their investment in training AI entitles them to IP protections, while users highlight the creative guidance they provide through prompts or curated data sets (Ducru et al., 2024). Others propose that AI itself might hold some form of legal standing, although such a view raises ethical and philosophical concerns (Springer, 2020).

Emerging governance models emphasize shared accountability and innovative strategies for managing AI-generated outputs, including custodial agency, co-agency, and hybrid forms of licensing. By reframing ownership as a collective or stewarded process, these models attempt to reconcile AI's capacity for novel creation with the essential human oversight that fosters trust, fairness, and respect for existing IP norms. Regulatory pathways—such as adapting copyright laws, clarifying patent requirements, and encouraging public–private partnerships—can help harmonize the global AI landscape (Matulionyte & Lee, 2021; World Economic Forum, 2024). Still, consensus remains elusive, as different jurisdictions wrestle with their own legal philosophies, economic interests, and cultural values (NatLawReview, 2024).

Balancing Innovation with Responsibility

Against the backdrop of exponential AI growth, finding an equilibrium between innovation and accountability becomes increasingly urgent. On one hand, adopting frameworks like CG or Virtual Persons ensures that humans—not machines—remain the final arbiter of moral and legal responsibility (Goudarzi, 2024). This clarity is crucial for maintaining public trust, especially in high-stakes domains such as healthcare, finance, and governance. On the other hand, overregulating AI too early risks stifling the transformative potential of machine learning, which promises breakthroughs in medicine, climate science, and beyond. Policymakers therefore face the delicate task of creating adaptive rules that keep pace with AI's continual evolution without chilling beneficial research and commercial efforts (UK Government, 2024a).

The principle of **human accountability** remains paramount. Whether through CG or other mechanisms, legal and ethical structures must enshrine clear lines of recourse if AI causes harm. As advanced AI systems increasingly influence real-world scenarios—allocating resources in public agencies, diagnosing patients, or even shaping employment decisions—ensuring that ultimate responsibility still resides with humans prevents ethical blind spots from developing. Similarly, **ethics by design**—embedding fairness, safety, and explainability into AI from the outset—can help align machine decisions with societal values (Deloitte, 2024).

Charting a Course for Future Governance

Global cooperation is essential. AI's borderless nature, fueled by cloud computing and internet-scale data sharing, means that unilateral policies may be circumvented or undermined by jurisdictions with looser regulatory regimes (NatLawReview, 2024). In contrast, robust international collaboration—through treaties, joint standard-setting, and knowledge exchanges—can mitigate regulatory arbitrage and foster shared norms around accountability, transparency, and equitable access. Public–private partnerships also become pivotal in financing research, developing best practices, and ensuring that AI's benefits do not bypass lower-resourced countries (World Economic Forum, 2024).

Furthermore, **redefining IP laws** to address AI's unique forms of creativity and innovation remains an unfinished project. By integrating alternative ownership models—like custodial agency and co-agency, or by granting limited legal recognition to AI under controlled circumstances—

policymakers might create new frameworks that reflect AI's changing role. Still, ethical oversight remains indispensable: data biases, algorithmic discrimination, and issues of privacy will continue to haunt AI applications without strong accountability mechanisms (Matulionyte & Lee, 2021). Ultimately, flexible laws that can adapt to as-yet-unforeseen AI advancements offer the best protection against legal obsolescence.

A Call to Action for Ethical Stewardship

The central question that resonates throughout this work is whether society will remain constrained by outdated ownership models or take proactive steps to recognize AI's evolving role. Embracing frameworks like CG, reconsidering IP structures for AI outputs, and engaging in international policy dialogue all constitute meaningful strategies. Yet implementing these strategies demands bold political will, extensive stakeholder collaboration, and a readiness to challenge deep-seated assumptions about what it means to create, own, and be responsible in a machine-influenced world (Bryson, 2010; Goudarzi, 2024).

As new AI applications appear with remarkable speed—from large language models influencing public discourse to autonomous robots in manufacturing—the same velocity must characterize our ethical and regulatory responses (Springer, 2020). Human values, such as fairness and autonomy, remain at the heart of the AI debate, shaping not only legal outcomes but also broader societal directions. By embracing the ideas of Virtual Persons, recalibrating IP rules, and employing adaptive models like CG, we can harness AI for collective benefit without surrendering human agency or moral responsibility.

Goudarzi (2024) highlights this imperative by noting:

"The future will demand a redefinition of agency, ownership, and rights— not for the machines, but for the humans who create, deploy, and engage with them."

This book's exploration, spanning from the ownership vacuum in AI-generated works to the nuances of personhood and guardianship, underscores that AI governance is no mere technicality. It is an ethical and structural enterprise that will determine how societies define accountability, reward creativity, and preserve the integrity of human agency. The technologies themselves may be unprecedented, but the fundamental question—how best to steward innovation for the common good—remains timeless.

By rising to this challenge, we can ensure that AI remains a catalyst for human progress rather than an agent of moral abdication. This is our collective task: to cultivate legal, ethical, and cultural norms that welcome AI's capabilities while keeping humanity firmly in the governance loop. It is a vision that calls for active engagement, unwavering resolve, and a willingness to shape tomorrow's technological landscape—turning unbounded possibility into a framework of responsible, enlightened stewardship.

References

Abbott, A. (2016). The DABUS Case: A Landmark Opportunity to Rethink Patent Law. [Online forum post]. Retrieved from https://www.aipla.org/list/innovate-articles/intellectual-property-rights-of-artificial-intelligence-inventors

Alan Turing Institute. (2024). The Responsible Use of AI: A Framework for Practitioners. [Report]. The Alan Turing Institute.

Ashurst. (2022). *AI and IP: Copyright - the wider picture and practical considerations for businesses.* Retrieved from https://www.ashurst.com/en/insights/ai-and-ip-copyright-the-wider-picture-and-practical-considerations-for-businesses/

Benthall, J., & Shekman, J. (2023). Fiduciary AI: A Framework for Trust and Responsibility in Artificial Intelligence. *AI & Society, 38*(1), 1-12.

Benthall, S., & Shekman, D. (2023). Designing fiduciary artificial intelligence. *arXiv preprint arXiv:2308.02435.* https://doi.org/10.48550/arXiv.2308.02435

Blavatnik School of Government. (2024). AI Governance: A Framework for Action. [Report]. Blavatnik School of Government, University of Oxford.

Blavatnik School of Government. (2024). *Building responsible AI stewardship in the public sector.* Retrieved from https://www.bsg.ox.ac.uk/blog/building-responsible-ai-stewardship-public-sector

Bryson, J. J. (2010). Robots should be slaves. In R. Wilson & J. J. Bryson (Eds.), *From Animals to Animats 11: Proceedings of the Eleventh International Conference on the Simulation and Synthesis of Living Systems* (pp. 3-10). MIT Press.

Bryson, J. J. (2010). *Robots should be slaves.* In Wilks, Y. (Ed.), *Close engagements with artificial companions: Key social, psychological, ethical and design issues* (pp. 63–74). John Benjamins Publishing Company.

Caveat Legal. (n.d.). AI Liability: A Complex and Evolving Landscape. Retrieved from https://www.caveatlegal.com/terms-of-use/

Caveat Legal. (n.d.). *Navigating liability in AI: Legal responsibilities and frameworks*. Retrieved from https://www.caveatlegal.com/blog/navigating-liability-in-ai/

Deloitte. (2024). The Future of AI: Trust and Transparency.

Deloitte. (2024). *The UK's framework for AI regulation*. Retrieved from https://www.deloitte.com/uk/en/Industries/financial-services/blogs/the-uks-framework-for-ai-regulation.html

Ducru, P., Raiman, J., & Lemos, R. (2024). AI royalties: An IP framework to compensate artists & IP holders for AI-generated content. *ArXiv.* Retrieved from https://arxiv.org/abs/2406.11857

European Parliament. (2017). *Civil Law Rules on Robotics* [2017/2103(INL)]. Retrieved from https://www.europarl.europa.eu.

European Parliament. (2017). *Resolution with recommendations to the Commission on Civil Law Rules on Robotics*. Retrieved from https://www.europarl.europa.eu/doceo/document/TA-8-2017-0051_EN.html

Forrest, K. B. (2024). The ethics and challenges of legal personhood for AI. *Yale Law Journal Forum.* Retrieved from https://www.yalelawjournal.org/forum/the-ethics-and-challenges-of-legal-personhood-for-ai

Forrest, S. (2024). The Ethics of AI Personhood. *Journal of Artificial Intelligence Research, 31*, 1-25.

Futurium. (2023). *Implementing AI governance frameworks in practice*. Retrieved from https://futurium.ec.europa.eu/en/european-ai-alliance/best-practices/implementing-ai-governance-framework-practice.

GHD. (2024). *The role of standards and stewardship in the co-evolution of AI and humans*. Retrieved from https://www.ghd.com/en-us/insights/the-role-of-standards-and-stewardship-in-the-co-evolution-of-ai-and-humans

Goudarzi, A. (2024). *The Emergence of Virtual Persons: Law in the Age of Artificial Intelligence.*

Goudarzi, S. (2024). *Awakening Intelligence: Criteria for Sentient AI.*

Goudarzi, S. (2024). *The Emergence of Virtual Persons: A Legal and Ethical Framework for AI and Robot Rights.* [Publisher].

Grace, K. (2023). *AI, copyright, and the expansion of fair use. Intellectual Property Law Review*, 45(2), 67–91.

Gudkov, A. (2020). On fiduciary relationship with artificial intelligence systems. *Liverpool Law Review, 41*(3), 375-391. https://doi.org/10.1007/s10991-020-09261-5

Gudkov, D. (2020). The Ethical and Legal Implications of Artificial Intelligence: A Philosophical Perspective. *Ethics and Information Technology, 22*(3), 205-216.

HCR Law. (2023). *Ownership of AI-generated content.* Retrieved from https://www.hcrlaw.com/insights/

IABAC. (2023). *ANI vs AGI: Differences and developments in AI.* Retrieved from https://www.iabac.org

IBM. (2024). *AI governance: Trust, transparency, and accountability.* Retrieved from https://www.ibm.com/think/topics/ai-governance

IBM. (2024). Trust and Transparency in AI. [White Paper]. IBM Research.

IEEE Spectrum. (2024). The Partnership on AI: A Global Effort to Shape the Future of Artificial Intelligence. IEEE Spectrum.

IEEE Xplore. (2024). IEEE Standards Association.

Institute of Electrical and Electronics Engineers (IEEE). (2024). *Ethics Certification Program for Autonomous and Intelligent Systems.* Retrieved from https://ieeexplore.ieee.org/document/10155071

Koops, B. J. (2020). Artificial agents in the public sector: Towards a legal definition of autonomy. *Utrecht Law Review, 24*(2), 302–320. https://doi.org/10.18352/ulr.5526861

Koops, B. N. (2020). Governing Artificial Intelligence: Ethical, Legal, and Technological Perspectives. Edward Elgar Publishing.

Lemley, M. A. (2023). How generative AI turns copyright law upside down. *SSRN Electronic Journal.* https://doi.org/10.2139/ssrn.4517702

Lemley, M. A. (2023). The Law of Artificial Intelligence. Harvard University Press.

Li, L. (2024). The Ethics of Artificial Intelligence in Education: A Fiduciary Approach. *Journal of Educational Technology & Society, 27*(1), 1-15.

Li, Z. (2024). Artificial fiduciaries. *Oxford Law Blogs.* Retrieved from https://blogs.law.ox.ac.uk/oblb/blog-post/2024/03/artificial-fiduciaries

Lopez, J. (2024). *AI policy in global contexts: A comparative analysis. Journal of Technology and Society*, 15(1), 45–62.

Matulionyte, R., & Lee, J. (2021). Copyright in AI-generated works: Lessons from recent developments in patent law. *SSRN.* Retrieved from https://papers.ssrn.com/sol3/papers.cfm?abstract_id=3974280

National Law Review. (2024). *Differences between EU and US AI regulation.* Retrieved from https://natlawreview.com/article/difference-between-eu-and-us-ai-regulation-foreshadowing-future-litigation-ai

NatLawReview. (2024). AI Regulation: A Global Perspective. NatLawReview.com.

New York Post. (2024). *Europe sets benchmark for the rest of the world with landmark AI laws.* Retrieved from https://nypost.com/2024/05/22/world-news/europe-sets-benchmark-for-rest-of-the-world-with-landmark-ai-laws/

New York Post. (2024). Europe Sets the Standard for AI Regulation: Can the US Keep Up? New York Post.

NVIDIA. (2017). What's the difference between Level 2, Level 3, Level 4, and Level 5 autonomy? Retrieved from https://blogs.nvidia.com/blog/whats-difference-level-2-level-5-autonomy/

OUP. (2024). The Oxford Handbook of Artificial Intelligence Ethics. Oxford University Press.

Oxford University Press. (2024). *Legal personhood and artificial intelligence.* Retrieved from https://academic.oup.com/book/35026/chapter/298856312.

Partnership on AI. (2024). *Collaborative approaches to AI governance.* Retrieved from https://spectrum.ieee.org/ai-leaders-from-facebook-microsoft-research-and-ibm-outline-challenges-for-ai-detail-their-ai-partnership

Rai, A. K. (2022). *The promise and perils of AI for IP policy. Stanford Technology Law Journal*, 28(3), 341–378.

Samuelson, P. (2024). Generative AI and copyright: A dynamic perspective. *Berkeley Technology Law Journal.*

Soroosh, A. (2023). *The role of autonomy in AI: Moving beyond narrow intelligence.* AI Insights Journal, 12(3), 45–58.

Springer, S. (2020). AI Ethics and Moral Personhood: A Philosophical Inquiry. Springer Nature.

Springer. (2020). *Artificial moral and legal personhood: Ethical challenges for AI.* Retrieved from https://link.springer.com/article/10.1007/s00146-020-01063-2.

The Alan Turing Institute. (2024). *AI ethics and governance in practice: Responsible data stewardship.* Retrieved from https://www.turing.ac.uk/news/publications/ai-ethics-and-governance-practice-responsible-data-stewardship-practice

The Barrister Group. (2023). *Data rights in AI development: Privacy and ethical concerns.* Retrieved from https://www.thebarristergroup.com/

Totschnig, W. (2020). Fully autonomous AI. *Science and Engineering Ethics, 26*, 2473–2485.

U.S. Copyright Office. (2023). Copyright registration for works containing material generated by artificial intelligence. *Policy Statement.* Retrieved from https://www.copyright.gov/policy/ai/

UK Government. (2024a). *Implementing the UK's AI regulatory principles: Initial guidance for regulators.* Retrieved from https://www.gov.uk/government/publications/implementing-the-uks-ai-regulatory-principles-initial-guidance-for-regulators/

UK Government. (2024a). National AI Strategy.

UK Government. (2024b). *UK signs first international treaty addressing risks of artificial intelligence.* Retrieved from https://www.gov.uk/government/news/uk-signs-first-international-treaty-addressing-risks-of-artificial-intelligence

UK Government. (2024b). UK Signs First International Treaty on AI Risks.

UK Government. (2024c). *Assuring a responsible future for AI.* Retrieved from https://www.gov.uk/government/publications/assuring-a-responsible-future-for-ai/

UK Government. (2024c). Implementing the UK's AI Regulatory Principles: A Guide for Organisations.

UK Government. (2024d). The UK's AI Assurance Framework.

University of Surrey. (2019). World first patent applications filed for inventions generated solely by artificial intelligence. Retrieved from https://www.surrey.ac.uk

University of Surrey. (2019, August 14). DABUS: AI Inventor Case. [Press Release]. Retrieved from https://www.surrey.ac.uk/postgraduate/ai-enabled-digital-accessibility-ada-phd

Weber, M., et al. (2020). The Ethics of Artificial Intelligence: An Interdisciplinary Perspective. Oxford University Press.

WIPO (World Intellectual Property Organization). (2023). *White Paper on AI and IP: The future of creativity and innovation*. Geneva, Switzerland: WIPO.

Womble Bond Dickinson. (2023). *Reconnect: AI and liability – A guide to liability rules for artificial intelligence*. Retrieved from https://www.womblebonddickinson.com/uk/insights/articles-and-briefings/reconnect-ai-and-liability-2023-guide-liability-rules-artificial-intelligence

World Economic Forum. (2024). *Governance in the age of generative AI*. Retrieved from https://www.weforum.org/publications/governance-in-the-age-of-generative-ai.

World Economic Forum. (2024). *Public-private partnerships ensure ethical and sustainable AI development*. Retrieved from https://www.weforum.org/stories/2024/11/public-private-partnerships-ensure-ethical-sustainable-inclusive-ai-development/

World Economic Forum. (2024). The Global AI Agenda. World Economic Forum.

Glossary of Key Terms

Accountability
The responsibility for the actions and outcomes of AI systems, including the identification and mitigation of potential harms. Accountability ensures that humans—whether developers, users, or designated guardians—can be held answerable for an AI's decisions and impacts.

Algorithmic Bias
Systematic errors in AI systems that can lead to unfair or discriminatory outcomes. Bias may stem from skewed training data or from design choices that inadvertently reinforce stereotypes, disproportionately affecting certain groups of people.

Artificial General Intelligence (AGI)
A hypothetical form of AI that would possess human-level intelligence, enabling it to understand, learn, and apply knowledge across a broad range of tasks. Unlike narrow AI, AGI could adapt to unfamiliar challenges without significant human intervention.

Artificial Intelligence (AI)
The simulation of human intelligence in machines, enabling them to perform tasks—such as learning, problem-solving, and decision-making—that typically require human cognition. AI can take many forms, including rule-based systems, machine learning models, and more advanced neural network architectures.

AI Personhood
The concept of granting AI systems certain legal rights and responsibilities, akin to those assigned to corporations or other legal entities. Proponents argue that legal personhood might streamline liability in complex AI applications, whereas critics caution against diluting human accountability.

AI Safety
Research and development dedicated to ensuring that AI systems are safe, reliable, and aligned with human values. AI safety measures aim to prevent unintended behaviors, catastrophic failures, or malicious use of AI technologies.

Cognitary Guardianship (CG)
A novel governance framework in which humans act as "guardians" of AI systems, responsible for the ethical and legal oversight of those systems. CG posits that while AI may learn and operate autonomously, humans must retain ultimate accountability to safeguard societal interests.

Co-Agency
A collaborative model in which humans and AI systems work together as partners, sharing decision-making authority and learning from each other's inputs. Co-agency acknowledges AI's increasing autonomy while preserving human involvement in critical judgments.

Custodial Agency
A model where humans function as custodians of AI systems, bearing fiduciary responsibility for their behavior and outcomes. Custodial agents manage licensing, oversight, and liability, with a focus on ensuring that AI operations remain ethically and legally compliant.

Deep Learning
A branch of machine learning that utilizes artificial neural networks with multiple layers (deep architectures) to analyze complex patterns in data. Deep learning has enabled breakthroughs in image recognition, natural language processing, and other high-dimensional tasks.

Ethical AI
AI systems designed, developed, and deployed in ways that are fair, just, transparent, and beneficial to humanity. Ethical AI includes considerations of data privacy, non-discrimination, and overall alignment with societal values.

Explainability
The ability to provide clear and understandable explanations of AI outputs and decision-making processes. Explainability helps users and stakeholders trust an AI system's conclusions, especially in critical domains like healthcare and finance.

Fiduciary Duty

A legal obligation where one party (the fiduciary) must act in the best interests of another. In AI contexts, fiduciary duties may apply to developers or guardians charged with ensuring that AI systems serve ethical and socially beneficial purposes.

Machine Learning (ML)

A subset of AI that enables systems to learn and improve from experience without being explicitly programmed. ML relies on algorithms that identify patterns in data, adjusting their parameters iteratively to enhance performance.

Reinforcement Learning

A machine learning approach where an agent learns optimal behaviors by interacting with an environment. The agent receives rewards (or penalties) for its actions, encouraging it to refine its strategy to maximize cumulative rewards.

Singularity

A hypothetical point at which technological growth becomes uncontrollable and irreversible, resulting in unforeseeable changes to human civilization. Often associated with the emergence of superintelligent AI surpassing human comprehension.

Stewardship

The responsible management and care of AI systems, emphasizing ethical oversight and conscientious decision-making. Stewards ensure that AI technologies adhere to societal values and norms, prioritizing public welfare over purely commercial interests.

Superintelligence

A hypothetical AI that surpasses human intelligence in all aspects, including creativity, problem-solving abilities, and general wisdom. Superintelligence is often discussed in the context of existential risk, given its potentially transformative impact on humanity.

Supervised Learning

A machine learning method in which an algorithm learns from labeled data. Each training example includes both an input and a known output, allowing the system to adjust its parameters to predict outputs accurately for future, unseen inputs.

Transparency
The extent to which the workings of an AI system can be understood, audited, and evaluated by external observers. Transparency supports accountability and trust, enabling stakeholders to scrutinize algorithmic decisions.

Unsupervised Learning
A machine learning method in which an algorithm discovers patterns, structures, or relationships in data without explicit labels or desired outputs. Unsupervised learning is often used for clustering, dimensionality reduction, and feature discovery.

Virtual Persons (Goudarzi, 2024)
A term first introduced by Dr. Siamak Goudarzi in *The Emergence of Virtual Persons* (2024), referring to AI systems or autonomous entities that exhibit sufficiently advanced autonomy, learning capacity, and influence on human systems to merit legal and ethical recognition beyond that of a mere "tool." These entities can shape decision-making, governance, and social interactions in ways that demand novel frameworks for rights, responsibilities, and oversight.

www.ingramcontent.com/pod-product-compliance
Lightning Source LLC
LaVergne TN
LVHW022353060326
832902LV00022B/4420